Death in a cold town

The Arlene Fraser case

Murder World

Scotland

Book 2

Murder World: Real crimes, real killers.

Table of Contents

Introduction 4
Prologue 10
Chapter 1: Falling in love 12
Chapter 2: Married bliss 19
Chapter 3: Attempted murder on Mother's Day 27
Chapter 4: Arlene vanishes 34
Chapter 5: A Detective Superintendent calls 38
Chapter 6: Hecky and the phantom Fiesta 48
Chapter 7: In court 58
Chapter 8: Doubts 67
Chapter 9: A free man 78
Chapter 10: Read my lips 85
Chapter 11: In court again 89
Conclusion 100
About the Author 114
Other Murder World Scotland books 115

Copyright © 2017 by Steve MacGregor - All rights reserved.

No part of this book or any portion thereof may be reproduced or transmitted in any form or by any means, electronic or mechanical, including photocopying, recording, or by any information storage and retrieval system without the written permission of the publisher, except where permitted by applicable law.

Introduction

It was a crisp, spring Tuesday morning as Michelle Scott walked up the drive towards the bungalow in which her friend, Arlene Fraser, lived. The two women had known each other since their schooldays and they often met up for lunch or just for a quick coffee. Michelle was worried about Arlene – the vivacious thirty-three year old had some problems in her life. She had health issues and, just four weeks before, on Mother's Day, Arlene had been so badly beaten and strangled by her husband that he had been arrested and charged with her attempted murder.

He had been forced to move out of the family home, leaving Arlene living there alone with their two young children. An injunction meant that he was no longer allowed to come to the house or to visit Arlene. One evening two weeks ago, Arlene had looked out of her window to see that her car was ablaze on the gravelled driveway outside the house. Insurance investigators concluded that the fire had been caused deliberately, though no-one had been charged with the crime. Michelle could still see the blackened patch on the drive as she walked up to the door.

She knocked several times, but there was no answer. That was odd because Arlene was very careful about keeping appointments and she had invited Michelle to come round at eleven o'clock, when the children would be at school. Michelle glanced at her watch. It was a few minutes after eleven. She tried the front door and found that it was unlocked. She opened the door and called out, but there was no response. That was very strange indeed – Arlene was extremely security conscious and never left the doors unlocked, even if she was stepping out for just a moment. Michelle cautiously entered the house and called out Arlene's name, but there was no response.

She looked around the small house. A vacuum cleaner stood in the middle the floor in Arlene's daughter's room. It was plugged in but switched off, as if Arlene had stopped cleaning for a moment and stepped away. Arlene's spectacles, contact lenses and medication were lying on her bedside table and her car keys were in the hallway. Most disconcertingly of all, the washing machine was running in the utility room. Michelle knew that Arlene had a phobia about fire and never, ever left the house while the washing machine was in operation.

Thoroughly worried now but unsure what she should do, Michelle left a note for Arlene saying that she'd be back later. Michelle came back several times that day, but each time she found the bungalow empty and no sign that Arlene had been there. At three o'clock that afternoon, Arlene's young daughter came home from school and was frightened and disconcerted to find that her mother wasn't there. Neighbours saw the little girl standing outside the house, crying, and took her in.

Arlene Fraser never did come home to her children, her family, her home or her friends. No trace of her, alive or dead, has ever been found. Her husband claimed that she must have gone away to start a new life with another man. The police had other ideas. Arlene's disappearance sparked one of the largest and longest running missing person enquiries ever undertaken and a murder investigation that would lead to the most contentious cases ever to come before the Scottish courts.

This is the story of Arlene Fraser, of what may have happened to her on April 28th 1998 and of the events which followed her disappearance.

***

The Moray coast in the north-east of Scotland is a cold place. Not in terms of the emotions or personalities of the inhabitants, but in a very literal way because the wind that constantly whips off the North Sea keeps temperatures down. The winters here are long, the days are short and most of the buildings are made of grey granite, which, as they huddle under a grey sky next to a grey sea makes any sensible person long for blue skies and sunshine. From

October to March, this is a place that's only suitable for the mentally and physically tough.

The town of Elgin lies in the heart of Moray, astride the busy A96 road which connects the cities of Aberdeen in the North-East and Inverness in the Central Highlands. In the normal course of things, some towns grow until they become cities. Elgin did the opposite, becoming a city in the thirteenth century when an imposing cathedral was built near the town centre and reverting to being a town again when the cathedral was de-consecrated during the reformation in the late 1500s. They like to do things differently here.

The High Street, Elgin

Photo: Colin Smith

This is prime farming country and for many years the local economy was based almost completely on agriculture. Since World War Two, the town has also benefited from the presence of two large military airbases nearby: Kinloss to the west and Lossiemouth to the north. These bases provided local people with work as well as providing a transient clientele for local businesses. Then, in the early 1970s, a huge oil rig fabrication yard intended to provide hardware for North Sea oil exploration was built in Ardersier, less than thirty miles to the west. This provided another boost for the town in terms of employment and attracting new residents. By the 1980s, Elgin was a thriving place with no shortage of work or prospects.

However , it wasn't just business that did well in Elgin – the town also became the social centre of Moray and an important location for the growth of the popular music scene in Scotland. The Two Red Shoes Ballroom was opened in 1960 by local entrepreneur and music promoter Albert Bonici. Tired of holding pop and beat music events in the town's draughty drill hall, Bonici built a new music venue in College Street where he managed to attract bands who would go on become some of the biggest in the business. The Beatles kicked off their first ever tour of the

UK in 1963 at this venue. The Who played here (Keith Moon was famously kicked out of a cafe in the town centre for misbehaving) as did Cream and Pink Floyd.

By the mid 1980s, when our story begins, the town was still thriving commercially, but was less successful in attracting well-known bands and once famous venues like the Two Red Shoes were falling into disrepair (by 1990, the Two Red Shoes had become a video rental shop). There was still a burgeoning social and music scene in the pubs of the town and no shortage of things to do on a Friday or Saturday night. Hogmanay in Elgin, as in most Scottish towns and cities, was a special night. There were parties galore and at midnight the dark winter skies over the Moray Firth were briefly illuminated by the sparkling and distant thunder of fireworks.

One young woman who was preparing to go to a party with friends on Hogmanay (New Year's Eve) 1985 had no idea that she would meet someone that evening who would change her life. Nor did she or anyone else know that she had just over thirteen years left to live and that her death would make her the subject of more than one of the most controversial and debated police investigations and murder trials in Scottish legal history.

Prologue

Securing a conviction for murder when there is no body is unusual, though it's not impossible as some murderers seem to think. Bringing the same person to trial twice for the same murder when there is no body must make this case unique in the annals of Scottish crime.

That makes this case interesting, but it's also makes it frustrating to write about. The lack of a body or definitive evidence of murder means that there are two opposing points of view here – there are those who feel that the evidence, circumstantial as it is, overwhelmingly suggests that the verdicts reached by the two trials are correct. However, there are those who just as vehemently believe the exact opposite – that the verdicts of the courts are a travesty which provided very little in the way of justice.

At least one book has been written about this case, it has generated countless articles in magazines and newspapers and it's a popular subject of discussion on Internet forums, but I am afraid that few of these are truly objective. Most take as their starting point a presumption of either innocence or guilt which considerably reduces their value as sources of information.

I will do my best to be objective in this book and to present the facts as they became known during the course of this case and in the lengthy court maneuverings which followed. Wherever possible, I have used evidence provided by witnesses as sworn testimony or recorded interviews and I have tried to tell the story chronologically. Of course, I too have a view on this case, but I'll keep that until the end of the book so that you can make up your own mind.

So, let's now travel back to the cold mid-winter of 1985/1986 and to Elgin where people are preparing for Hogmanay celebrations...

Chapter 1: Falling in love

January 1985 – May 1986

At Hogmanay 1985, people all over Scotland were preparing to celebrate the New Year in the traditional way – with parties, music, dancing and not a few drinks. 1985 had been a mixed year in many ways. In the UK, inflation was a continuing problem and the average house value was up to £40,000 and petrol had reached the shocking price of £1.80 per gallon. The miner's strike ended with a victory for Margaret Thatcher's government and the closure of more coal mines. In the wider world, the Italian cruise liner Achille Lauro was hi-jacked by Palestinian terrorists and an elderly passenger was murdered, a wall collapsed during the European Cup Final at the Heysel Stadium in Brussels killing thirty-nine fans and a volcanic eruption near the town of Armero in Columbia killed 25,000 people. But it wasn't all bad news in 1985: the Live Aid concert in July raised millions of pounds to help charities in Africa, the Soviet Union had a new leader, Mikhail Gorbachev, who seemed to offer some hope of an end to the armed stand-off between east and west and in the UK, comedian Ernie Wise made the very first mobile telephone call.

Photo: Love Maegan

Top movies of the year included *Back to the Future*, *The Color Purple* and Roger Moore's last outing as James Bond, *A View to a Kill*. In music, the big acts included Duran Duran, Simple Minds, Dire Straits, Madonna and Phil Collins. On television, people were still uncertain about a new BBC soap called *Eastenders*, Colin Baker was the sixth *Dr Who* and the much loved sit-com *Are You Being Served* finally ended after thirteen years. In terms of fashion, people were wearing bat-wing jumpers, shoulder pads, fingerless mittens and berets and big hair was cool.

In Elgin, twenty-one year old Arlene McInnis was getting ready for a Hogmanay night-out with her friends. Arlene was slim, attractive and had the requisite eighties big blonde hair which she carefully back-combed before applying lots of make-up. Arlene was popular but she was also a rebel and a woman of firm beliefs who wasn't afraid to share them. That didn't endear her to some people who still felt that a woman's role was to be demure and retiring, but Arlene enthusiastically embraced the new freedoms which had come with the eighties.

Under the confident and rebellious exterior, many people who knew Arlene well understood that this was partly a manifestation of her lack of confidence. Most people regarded her as extremely attractive but Arlene didn't really believe that, didn't feel that she had anything worthwhile or interesting to say and was secretly amazed when men showed an interest in her. It seems very likely that her combative attitude was at least in part an unconscious emotional pre-emptive strike, designed to keep other people at arm's-length so that they couldn't hurt her.

Some men found Arlene's aggressive and confrontational approach off-putting. Attitudes towards woman and particularly towards what was regarded as permissible behavior for women had changed greatly since World War Two. However, a willingness to challenge men's views was still regarded by many folk as an unsuitable thing for a woman to do, especially one who might be looking for a husband. Some of her friends and family told Arlene that she should try to act a little, well, more like a lady. She laughed and carried on just as she was.

At school, partly because of her attitude, Arlene hadn't done well. Her teachers agreed that this certainly wasn't because she was unintelligent, it was just that she couldn't seem to generate sufficient enthusiasm to focus on studying for any of her subjects. She was constantly and unfavorably compared at school to her elder sister Carol who had done well at just about everything including finding boyfriends. By 1985, Carol was married and had moved to Erskine, just outside Glasgow, with her husband Stephen Gillies. Arlene stayed in Elgin with her father Hector (her parents were separated) and found work in a fashion shop in the centre of town.

On Hogmanay 1985 Arlene spent a large part of the evening with twenty-six year old Nathaniel (Nat) Fraser. The two had met in passing before at other social events, but they seemed to particularly hit it off this evening. Nat was a burly, handsome man and a partner in a successful fruit and vegetable business in Elgin as well as being the guitarist in popular local band The Minesweepers and a player for Elgin rugby team. He was cheery, affable, confident and generally well liked. He was never short of money though he always seemed to be up to something to make a little extra cash and many people described him as *"a bit of a Jack-the-lad"*. He did have a propensity, after a few drinks, to emphasize his side of an argument with his fists, but that wasn't unusual enough to be remarkable. In the eighties, alcohol fuelled violence wasn't just tolerated in Scottish men, it was to some degree expected. Nat was also very popular with the female population of Elgin, though he seemed to favor quiet, compliant women - some people were surprised that he took an interest in feisty Arlene.

Relationships are odd things and almost never easy to analyze or understand from the outside. Such was the case with the intense relationship which quickly developed between Nat Fraser and Arlene McInnis. Nat went through girlfriends quickly and often concurrently – to most people he appeared to regard women as nothing more than commodities to be assessed, inspected, used and discarded as required, just like the fruit and vegetables he bought and sold. Despite this, he seemed genuinely and completely besotted with Arlene. Arlene too seemed completely swept off her feet by Nat, by his attention and the frequent presents he gave her.

Despite this, many of her friends and family warned Arlene to stay away from Nat, including her older sister Carol. Fraser was unreliable, they told her, untrustworthy where women were concerned and a man who would never settle down. Ignoring this well-meaning advice, Arlene began to spend increasing amounts of time with Nat. Four months later, she moved into his bungalow at Number 2 Smith Street in New Elgin, a group of houses which had formerly been a separate village to the south of the main part of the town.

Taylor and Fraser Fruit and Vegetables, the business Nat ran with his friend and partner Ian *'Pedro'* Taylor who he had known since they attended school together, was doing well. Both men were making reasonable money though Taylor, like Nat, always seemed to be looking for additional ways of making extra cash – he generally had one or two cars for sale at any given time and his enthusiasm for wheeling and dealing led to his acquiring the nickname *'Del Boy'*, after the lead character in the popular television show *Only Fools and Horses*.

After Arlene moved in with him, Nat continued to make daily fruit and vegetable deliveries around Elgin and the surrounding area in the Taylor and Fraser van and Arlene continued to work as an assistant in the clothes shop in the centre of town. The two lived together without major issues and in September 1986 they announced that they would be getting married in May the following year in the town's South Church, a massive, Gothic building in the town centre. Nat gave Arlene an expensive sapphire engagement ring which she proudly wore. They planned a large, formal wedding and reception to which large numbers of friends and family would be invited. Ian Taylor agreed to be Nat's Best Man.

To the surprise of some, it seemed that Arlene and Nat were well settled together and when in late 1986 Arlene discovered that she was pregnant, well, that appeared to be a welcome and happy development, even if it did happen a few months before the planned wedding.

Chapter 2: Married bliss

May 1986 – March 1998

Things didn't go entirely smoothly for the happy couple in the run-up to their wedding. Just two weeks before, Arlene overheard Nat making a phone call. As she later tearfully told her father, she believed that Nat was making a date to see another woman. Fraser vehemently denied it, but the call provoked a massive argument which culminated in Arlene storming out, moving back to her father's house and wondering whether all those people who had warned her about her future husband's womanising were right? She considered whether she should call off the wedding?

But, she was pregnant with Nat Fraser's baby, he swore that she was mistaken and that he hadn't been making a date with another woman, and anyway, he said, it would never happen again. After two days Arlene moved back to the bungalow in Smith Street and agreed to the wedding going ahead.

On the evening before the wedding Nat, Ian Taylor and a group of friends were out on the town in Elgin for Nat's Stag Night. Everybody had a great deal to drink and it all seemed to be very convivial when suddenly, Nat became involved in a brawl. Afterwards, no-one who was there could remember specifically who was involved or what had provoked the punch-up. No-one seemed particularly surprised or perturbed either – it wasn't the first time that Nat had been involved in an argument that had become physical.

Arlene on her wedding day

Photo: The Northern Scot

Arlene turned up at the church the next day in a white Rolls-Royce and wearing a white satin bridal gown. She was accompanied by her father and everyone agreed that she looked stunning. Nat turned up wearing his kilt, two black eyes and a badly bruised nose and nursing a hangover of monumental proportions. Everyone agreed that he looked awful. Somehow, Nat got through the service and the exchange of rings and vows – he gave Arlene an expensive gold and diamond wedding ring. By the time of the reception in the evening, Nat had recovered sufficiently to play Eric Clapton's *Wonderful Tonight* with The Minesweepers.

Three months later, Arlene gave birth to a son, Jamie. She and Nat were overjoyed and the Fraser household settled down into what appeared from the outside to be a state of connubial bliss. However, on the inside, things didn't look quite so rosy.

Part of the problem was Nat's insistence on continuing to play with the band. He worked long hours, six days a week for the fruit and vegetable business, but he also continued to play guitar with The Minesweepers. Most weekends the band gigged at parties and weddings and Nat often didn't get home until the early hours of the morning. There were rumours that Nat was seeing other women but when Arlene remonstrated, he denied this. Arlene begged him to stay at home with her and Jamie. Nat refused. He said that he had to continue to play with the band because they needed the money – he wanted to provide for his wife and child and he was still building up the fruit and vegetable business.

Arlene began to feel increasingly isolated and lonely. She had given up her job at the shop in town when they married, but being at home with a young child meant that it was also difficult for her to see her friends. This seemed to suit Nat who preferred his wife to be at home looking after their child. Despite his frequent absences until the early hours of the morning and continuing rumours of his infidelity, Nat was very jealous of Arlene and didn't approve of her going out without him. On the rare occasions when she was able to meet up with friends in an evening, he criticised her for dressing provocatively, saying that she didn't need to dress like that if she was simply going out with female friends. Gradually, Arlene began to lose touch with her friends and to spend more and more of her time at home with Jamie in the bungalow in Smith Street.

Then, less than one year after they were married, Arlene met seventeen year old Dougie Green, the van boy who worked with Nat on his delivery rounds. Green was young, unattached, handsome and fun. He was clearly attracted to Arlene and began to visit the house to see her when Nat was out gigging with the band. One evening, after a few drinks, the two ended up in bed together.

Nat found out about the one-night stand and he was incandescently angry, though most of his anger seemed to be directed at Arlene and not at Dougie Green. There were a series of angry confrontations between Arlene and Nat. Nat's anger began to show the first signs of turning to physical violence - he began pushing her and she confided to her family that sometimes she was afraid of him. Nothing was resolved by these arguments and Nat was left even more suspicious and jealous than before. On more than one occasion he secretly followed Arlene when she went out to spend the evening with friends so that he could be certain that she wasn't meeting with another man.

In 1990, Nat's suspicions finally spilled over into real violence. Arlene came home after a night out with friends to find Nat waiting angrily for her – for some reason he was certain that she had been with another man. He ripped her clothes off, slapped and punched her and then kicked her in the stomach as she lay on the ground. Arlene was sufficiently frightened that she fled to a women's refuge where she stayed for ten days, taking Jamie with her. She also contacted a lawyer and asked about divorce. Nat seemed contrite and very apologetic. He had lost his temper, he explained, only because he loved her so much that he couldn't bear the thought of her being with another man. It would never happen again. He sent flowers, jewellery and romantic cards to her at the refuge. Eventually, she agreed to move back to Smith Street.

In 1992, Arlene had a second child, Natalie, but the underlying problems in the marriage continued. As before, the main issue was Nat's jealousy which was focussed on any occasion when Arlene went out without him. Arlene didn't get the chance to go out alone very often, but when she did, she loved spending time with her friends and wasn't willing to give these evenings up. There were frequent arguments, several of which became physical, though not to the same extent as had happened in 1990. Things were so bad that, between 1992 and 1997, Arlene went to see her solicitor three more times. Each time she told her that she had decided to divorce Nat. But each time she changed her mind when Nat apologised for his behaviour. In 1995, Nat gave Arlene an expensive gold eternity ring as part of making up after yet another argument.

During this period Arlene also developed Crohn's disease, a painful and debilitating inflammatory bowel disease associated with long-term stress. The disease is incurable and it can have life-threatening complications, but Arlene took medication which helped to keep the disease under control. The stress of frequent fights with Nat caused the disease to flare-up on several occasions and Arlene steadily lost weight.

In 1997, Arlene enrolled in a part-time, two year business studies course at Moray College, a further education institution in Elgin. Her plan was to learn sufficient skills that she could become financially independent from Nat if she chose. Up until then, Nat had brought all the money into the household and had given Arlene an allowance. She had made no money of her own since she had left her job in the clothes shop. Recognising that this gave Nat control over her, Arlene was determined to find ways of making her own money.

At around the same time, she spent £3,000 that she had somehow managed to save from her allowance on a breast augmentation operation. Nat knew nothing about the operation beforehand and it seems that this was another way for Arlene to re-asserting control over her own life and improving her self-esteem.

Predictably, Nat reacted badly to news of the operation. He saw it as another example of Arlene trying to make herself attractive to other men. He began shredding her clothes so that she couldn't go out with her friends. If this didn't work, he took to hiding her contact lenses and glasses. On one occasion, when she suggested that it might be best if they slept in separate beds, he poured water over the spare bed, forcing her to share a bed with him. His behaviour towards her became increasingly erratic and unpredictable. In February 1998, Nat beat Arlene so brutally about the face and jaw that she was unable to eat. Her weight dropped to just seven stone and she became withdrawn and depressed. She told Michele Scott, a friend from her schooldays, that not only did she not love Nat any more, she was also frightened of him.

It was agreed that Nat would move out of the house for a month and that he would go to live with his friend Hector *'Hecky'* Dick who owned a farm at Mosstowie, just outside Elgin. Fraser and Dick had become friends while attending Elgin Academy and often went drinking together. In the event, Nat stayed away from Arlene for less than one week and neighbours noticed that he seemed to be at the house on Smith Street more often during this week than when he was actually supposed to be living there.

Finally, Arlene relented and agreed that Nat could move back in, on the understanding that, if there was any further violence, the marriage was over. It was also agreed that, though the two would continue to live together as man and wife, they would lead quite separate lives. Arlene would continue with her Business Studies course with the intention of finding a job when she qualified. She would also continue to go out with her friends as and when she chose. Nat wasn't happy with this, but Arlene made it clear that the alternative was divorce and so he agreed. For a short time, things in Smith Street were calm.

Chapter 3: Attempted murder on Mother's Day

March 1998

On Mother's Day, Sunday 22nd March 1998, Arlene went out for the evening with a group of three female friends. After the bar in which they had been drinking closed, they all went back to Michele Scott's house in New Elgin and continued drinking there. Arlene didn't arrive back at Smith Street until 05:30 am to find Nat waiting for her. A violent argument ensued which ended with Nat beating Arlene and then strangling her to the point that she passed out and fell unconscious to the floor.

Arlene in 1997

She came to and Nat told her that she had collapsed

following some kind of fit and denied that he had attacked her. The following morning Arlene realised that her eyes and eyelids looked odd – they were swollen and covered with small red dots. When Nat went to work, Arlene went to see her doctor. The doctor explained that the red dots in and around her eyes and eyelids were petechiae, broken capillary blood vessels caused by strangulation. He also pointed out that he had only heard of such things before on the dead bodies of strangling victims and that Arlene herself must have been very close to death. He also found severe bruising on Arlene's shoulder, back, upper chest and arm.

The doctor urged Arlene to go to the police and finally, reluctantly, she agreed. She explained what had happened and the police arranged for her to be examined by another doctor. The petechiae in and around her eyes were so unusual in a living person that the police also had her examined by a pathologist – the only medical practitioner they could find with experience of this sort of injury. He confirmed that Arlene must have come very close to being killed by her husband.

As a result, Nat Fraser was immediately arrested and charged with attempted murder. Arlene was horrified – she didn't want her children's father to end up in jail and she had only wanted him kept away from her. She tried to back away from the charge, but it was too late. When Nat was released on bail, he was placed under an injunction which meant that he was not allowed to approach the house in Smith Street or Arlene. He went to stay with his business partner Ian Taylor in the village of Lhanbryde, four miles from Elgin.

Arlene went back to see her solicitor and this time, she assured her, she would go through with it – she would divorce Nat on the grounds of his continuing violence towards her. There was extended discussion of what sort of financial settlement she wanted. Arlene told her solicitor that Nat had offered her £30,000 as a final settlement, and warned that if she did not accept this offer, he would give her nothing at all. The solicitor explained that it was usual in these cases to begin with a high claim and then to allow this to be reduced during negotiation. It was agreed that, in view of Nat's business interests and property, the initial claim would be for a settlement of £250,000.

From the time he had been arrested, it was clear that Nat saw himself as the injured party. Everything was Arlene's fault – it was her fault that she had stayed out late which made him angry enough to attack her and it was her fault that the police were involved. When he was released on bail, he ominously told Arlene that he would never forget what she had done to him, conveniently forgetting what he had done to her. When he discovered that Arlene not only intended to divorce him but that she was demanding a large settlement, he became extremely angry. Arlene told one of her friends, Marion Taylor that Nat had said to her: *"If you are not going to live with me, you will not be living with anyone."*

Nat Fraser had another reason for being very nervous about any kind of police or formal scrutiny of his affairs in early 1998. Although the fruit and vegetable business was doing well, Nat was also the partner in another, clandestine business with Hector Dick. Nat and Hector were involved in selling smuggled alcohol obtained from a gang based in Fife.

The level of duty charged on alcohol in the UK is much higher than that charged in most European countries – that's why there are strict limits on how much alcohol and tobacco you are permitted to bring into the UK. In the early 1990s, smugglers were bringing vast quantities of alcohol purchased in Europe in the UK hidden in trucks and cars. No-one is really sure how much bootleg booze was brought into the UK in this way, but it has been estimated that this was costing the UK Government anything up to £100 million each year in lost revenue.

Alcohol smuggled into the UK in this way could be sold on at prices well below those charged by legitimate sellers but which still provided handsome profits for the smugglers. By the mid 1990s, many organized groups which had previously been involved in smuggling drugs switched to alcohol smuggling – the profit margins were almost as great but the penalties much less if they were caught. By 1998, it was estimated that over one million smuggled pints of beer were being sold in the UK every single day!

However, the largest profits weren't in the smuggling of beer or wine, they were in the smuggling of spirits. All that was needed was a distribution network capable of selling the bootleg spirits on to members of the public. That was where Hector Dick and Nat Fraser came in. They weren't directly involved in the smuggling, but they were both selling on large quantities of spirits for the gang in Fife, with Nat using his fruit and vegetable deliveries as a cover for the sale of smuggled spirits. The last thing that Nat Fraser wanted was the police looking in detail at his affairs, or an inquisitive solicitor demanding a close look at his finances – Arlene knew all about his bootlegging activities.

Nat had been forced to leave Arlene with his prized car, a black Ford Granada with the personalized number plate A19 NAT, at the house in Smith Street after the attack. The terms of the injunction against him meant that he was not allowed access to the car which Arlene had started using. Nat made several efforts to persuade Arlene to let him have the car, but she refused. On the evening of 5th April, two weeks after the attack, Arlene became aware of a commotion outside the bungalow. She looked out and saw that the car, which was parked in the driveway, was ablaze. The fire brigade were called and the fire was put out but the car was completely destroyed. Insurance assessors initially concluded that an electrical fault had caused the fire but a more detailed examination showed that it had been deliberately started. The identity of the arsonist was never established, but there were many who thought that Nat Fraser must have been involved. It was assumed that he felt the same about his car as he apparently did about his wife – if he couldn't have it, no-one would.

Arlene spent more time with her solicitor, Ms Loane Lennon, discussing the terms of the divorce. They agreed to communicate their request for a financial settlement to Nat Fraser's solicitor and Arlene made an appointment to meet Ms Lennon on the afternoon of Tuesday 28th April to discuss progress and to finalise the paperwork. Tuesdays were the only weekdays on which Arlene didn't have to go into Moray College to study, and she often used these days to catch up with friends - she also invited her friend Michelle Scott round on the 28th for lunch.

When Nat heard that Arlene was planning to ask for a settlement of £250,000 he was aghast – he believed that the most he could possibly raise was £50,000. There were also other circumstances of which Arlene was unaware – for example, he had told her (and most other people) that he had a mortgage on the property in Smith Street, whereas the truth was that he owned it outright and there never was a mortgage. It was inevitable that this would become known if there was any form of investigation into his financial affairs which might make him liable for an even larger settlement.

It must also have crossed Nat Fraser's mind that, if he refused Arlene's financial demands, she could threaten to reveal details of his income from the bootleg spirit business to the police or to the Revenue and Customs Service. Nat was in a very difficult position – Arlene had made it clear that she wouldn't have him back in any circumstances, but he simply couldn't afford a divorce.

Chapter 4: Arlene vanishes

April 28th, 1998

Tuesday 28th April 1998 was a beautiful, clear spring day. At around 08:15 Arlene Fraser was seen by a neighbour hanging up washing in the garden of the bungalow on Smith Street. At approximately 08:50 she was seen by another neighbour at her front door, waving to ten year old Jamie and five year old Natalie as they left together on their short walk to nearby New Elgin Primary School. Jamie was particularly excited that day as he was to travel with a group of children from the area to attend an anti-litter event in Inverness. At 09:41 a telephone call at the school was logged from Arlene asking what time Jamie would be returning from Inverness? A clerical assistant took the call and said that she would find out and call back. That was the last time that anyone is known to have spoken to Arlene and when approximately ten minutes later the school called her back, there was no reply.

Smith Street, looking from Main Street. Number 2 is on the right.

Photo: Google Streetview

At 11:00 Michelle Scott arrived for her lunch date with Arlene. There was no answer when she knocked. When she tried the door, it was unlocked – Arlene was very security conscious after the house had been burgled in the early 1990s and she never left the door unlocked. Concerned, Michelle entered the house, calling to Arlene, but there was no-one there. Michelle looked briefly round the house and noted that the vacuum cleaner was standing in the middle of Natalie's room, plugged in but switched off as if Arlene had been interrupted while cleaning her daughter's room. Even more worrying, the washing machine was still running

– Arlene also had a phobia about washing machines causing fires and generally never left the machine running when she was out of the house for longer than a few minutes.

Michelle looked around and saw that Arlene's contact lenses, glasses, Crohn's disease medication and expensive watch were all on a bedside cabinet. An open make-up bag lay on the bed and a pot of foundation with the lid off sat on the dressing table. The only thing that appeared to be missing was Arlene's favourite three-quarter length, faux-leather brown coat. Feeling very uneasy, Michelle left and phoned several times over the next couple of hours. There was no reply and when she returned briefly to the house at 1:00pm, there was still no sign of Arlene and everything was just as it had been during her earlier visit. Michelle left a note asking Arlene to call her as soon as possible.

Meanwhile, Nat Fraser had arrived at work as usual at around 07:30 am that morning before leaving in the Taylor and Fraser van to deliver fruit and vegetables round Elgin. Unusually, he took a van boy with him on this particular morning – in recent years he generally preferred to undertake the deliveries alone. Shortly after 09:00, he broke off from making deliveries to make a call from a telephone box in the centre of Elgin. He called Hazel Walker, a young woman who lived in nearby Fochabers and who was the niece of one of the other members of The

Minesweepers. He had arranged to call her the previous day and he remained on the phone chatting with her for around forty minutes before continuing with his deliveries.

Back in Smith Street, at just after 3:00pm Arlene's neighbours Irene Higgins and her husband Graham noticed that Natalie was outside the house and appeared to be distressed. Irene spoke to the little girl who explained that her mother wasn't there. The Higgins, who had looked after Natalie before, took her to their house and watched for Arlene's return. Instead, at 20:00 Michelle Scott arrived, by now very worried indeed. She and Irene Higgins went in to the house and looked around. There was still no sign of Arlene and the house was just as before except that there was now a note on the hall floor. It was from Jamie and read: *"I was home at 7.30pm. You not in. Round at Mark's. Where are you!"* Un-noticed by the Higgins, Jamie had come home, found that his mother wasn't there and had left a note for her before going round to a friend's house.

When the two women went back to the Higgin's house, they explained what they had found to Graham Higgins. After a great deal of discussion, he agreed to call the police to report their concerns about Arlene. In doing so, he launched one of the biggest and longest running cases ever undertaken by Grampian Police.

Chapter 5: A Detective Superintendent calls

April 1998 – December 1998

Grampian Police were formed in 1975 in a merger between Aberdeen City Police and the Scottish North Eastern Counties Constabulary. The force covered not just the city of Aberdeen and towns such as Nairn, Forres and Elgin but also the North Sea where they had overall responsibility for crimes committed on permanent oil and gas platforms. Grampian Police ceased to exist as an independent force in 2013 when all Scottish Police services were amalgamated as Police Scotland. When Graham Higgins called in to report Arlene Fraser missing on April 28th 1998 it was Grampian Police he contacted and from the outset, they treated her disappearance as something much more sinister than a simple missing person case.

The circumstances of her disappearance were themselves concerning – for a woman who was known to be a loving and caring mother to abandon her two young children is very unusual and when this was coupled with the fact that, less than five weeks before, her estranged husband had been charged with her attempted murder, then it was always likely that the police would take the view that this not a simple case of a woman who had run away.

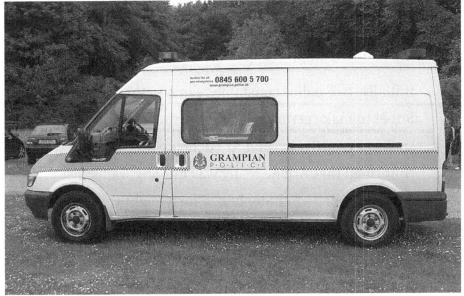

Photo: Dave Connor

There was another reason that Grampian police officers were likely to take a missing person case very seriously indeed in the spring of 1998. In the summer of 1997, nine year old Scott Simpson was reported missing by his parents in Aberdeen. Grampian Police officers undertook a search for the boy, but found no trace of him. Just five days later, Scott's body was discovered in an area supposedly searched by the police. He had been abducted and murdered by a paedophile. The murderer was finally arrested and sent to prison, but Grampian Police came under intense scrutiny and an independent report criticised the over-casual way in which the force had reacted to the initial report of the missing boy. On 24th April, just four days before Arlene went missing, Dr Ian Oliver, the Chief Constable of Grampian Police, resigned partly as a result of criticism of the force's handling of the search for the missing boy.

Initially, two police constables came to the house in Smith Street to make certain that Arlene wasn't there. They also spoke to the Higgins and to Michele Scott. When it was confirmed that Arlene really was missing, Detective Superintendent Jim Stephen, a forty-eight year old burly, veteran detective who had joined Grampian Police when it was formed in 1975, was assigned to the case. Given the timing, it probably isn't surprising that from the very start DS Stephen made absolutely certain that no-one could accuse him of being over-casual about this missing person case.

From the moment that he was allocated the case, DS Stephen believed that he knew what had happened to Arlene. In a later interview with the Telegraph newspaper he noted:

> *"From early on, we all felt that this was not a missing persons inquiry - it was a murder. But because we couldn't find the body, there was no crime scene and no forensic evidence. All we had to go on was some circumstantial hints."*

Nat Fraser's alibi for the 28th April was unassailable. Even that fuelled DS Stephen's suspicions – as far as he was concerned, innocent people rarely had such a comprehensive alibi. Stephen believed that Fraser's actions, including the taking of a van boy on the delivery round when he usually did not and the lengthy telephone call at the very time that Arlene was thought to have gone missing, were a deliberate attempt to build an alibi for himself while a confederate was abducting Arlene. When he discovered that the public telephone box in Elgin at which Fraser had made the call to Hazel Walker was one of the few in town covered by CCTV cameras and that a time-stamped video existed showing Fraser making the call, he was even more certain that Fraser's actions that morning were part of an elaborate charade intended to make it obvious that he could not have abducted Arlene.

The first police officers to arrive at Smith Street had been two constables based in Elgin who were alerted by Graeme Higgin's call: PC Neil Lynch and PC Julie Clark. They arrived late in the evening of 28th April and looked around the house to assure themselves that Arlene was indeed missing. They returned several times that night to check that she hadn't returned but it wasn't until the following day, April 29th, that Grampian Police officers conducted a detailed examination of the bungalow on Smith Street. They found no evidence of a disturbance or foul play and they took detailed video recordings of the interior and exterior of the house. They also confirmed that Arlene's spectacles, contact lenses and medication were still there, as were her passport, driving licence and keys.

On Sunday 3rd May, Grampian Police called for volunteers to assist in a search of open spaces in and around Elgin. Over three hundred people assisted, including Arlene's father and step-father. Nat Fraser didn't take part.

When officers from Grampian Police began interviewing witnesses in Elgin, they discovered that most people believed that Arlene had simply gone on holiday. There were also persistent rumours that she was taking drugs, seeing other men and drinking excessively. For these reasons, some people were very sympathetic to Nat Fraser and resented the fact that the police seemed to be treating him like a potential criminal. DS Stephen was certain that Nat Fraser himself was the source of the rumours blackening Arlene's character. He later said:

> *"He peddled the propaganda - that she was seeing other men, she was involved in drugs, she was a bad mother and didn't look after the house. All of these things were unfounded, but we were carrying out investigations in a public opinion that was very pro-Nat and anti-Arlene."*

From the very beginning, Nat Fraser made it clear that he was happy to assist Grampian Police in any way that he could and that he wanted Arlene found. Graham Higgins had called him at Ian Taylor's house on the evening of 28th April to tell him that Arlene was missing. He discussed with Taylor whether he should visit hospitals in the area to ask if they had seen Arlene? Taylor advised him that it would be better to let the police handle the investigation.

Nat made a point of learning the first names of all the senior officers involved in the case and he would toot the horn of his delivery van and wave if he saw them while he was making deliveries. He also frequently called in at the Police Station in Elgin to ask whether there had been any progress in the case? In early June he talked to the press for the first time and made a televised appeal, not for information about what had happened to his wife, but directly to her:

> *"My message to Arlene is to come home because the children are missing you terribly."*

Nat Fraser during the televised appeal to Arlene

He continued to claim that he believed that Arlene was still alive, but that for some reason she had decided to disappear. He hinted to those who would listen that she might have done this in order to direct suspicion at him while she was living in secret with a new lover. He also told the police that there had been two stashes of money in the house amounting to several hundred pounds. One had been hidden behind an air-vent in Arlene's bedroom and the other had been in a locked gun cabinet in the loft. He claimed that both were missing and suggested that Arlene had used this cash to fund her disappearance.

Grampian Police remained convinced that Arlene Fraser was dead and a great deal of time and effort was put into proving this. In Scotland, the Presumption of Death (Scotland) Act of 1977 provides a mechanism whereby a person may be legally declared dead even where their body is not found (a similar Act was introduced in England and Wales in 2014). Grampian Police used guidance contained in this Act to pursue a legal presumption that Arlene Fraser was dead, an essential prerequisite if they were to seek a murder conviction.

Police officers took over 2,500 statements from witnesses and over 4,000 names were logged into HOLMES (Home Office Large Major Enquiry System), a UK-wide police IT system which allowed the storage and comparison of data. One officer, Constable Gordon Ritchie, began what was, at the time, the longest and most detailed *"presumption of death"* enquiry ever undertaken by a UK police force. Ritchie contacted banks and financial institutions, government agencies and the NHS across the UK. If Arlene Fraser tried to open a bank account, claim any benefits, order any paperwork such as a new driving license or passport or if she saw a doctor or tried to obtain a prescription for glasses or contact lenses or if she was stopped by the police or any border agency, Grampian Police would immediately be informed.

In October 1998, Grampian Police issued a fresh appeal for information, noting that they believed that Arlene Fraser was dead and that she had been the victim of *"something criminal"*. As a result of this appeal, Constable Ritchie took a further 43 witness statements. Constable Ritchie's work was so comprehensive that it has since been used by other UK police services as a template for this type of enquiry. Due to his efforts, if Arlene Fraser was alive and undertook almost any form of activity that involved contact with a government agency, alarms would sound. But none did. After 28th April 1998, there was no record of Arlene making any form of contact with any official agency or other institution anywhere in the UK. As time passed, this seemed to confirm that Arlene Fraser was indeed dead.

The police also made strenuous efforts to locate her body. RAF aircraft from the nearby base at Kinloss were asked to overfly the area in a search for potential burial sites. A forensic archeologist from Aberdeen University was consulted and Strathclyde Police loaned Roscoe and Sabre, two police dogs trained to search for human remains. Officers from Derbyshire Police who had helped set up the CATCHEM (Centralised Analytical Team Collating Homicide Expertise and Management) IT system which was designed to collate and analyze data about offenders also travelled to Elgin to assist.

The result of all this effort was absolutely nothing. There was no sign of Arlene alive but neither was there any forensic evidence that she had been murdered or any sign of her body. The case was in danger of losing impetus when, in

December 1998, the police finally received some interesting information from an unexpected source.

Chapter 6: Hecky and the phantom Fiesta

December 1998 – April 2002

A witness came forward to say that, while drinking in a pub in Elgin, he had overheard a conversation which seemed to relate to Arlene's disappearance. He had heard a man discussing how he had sold a car to a friend of Nat Fraser just before the disappearance, but that he had been paid not to talk about it.

Police enquiries identified the person overheard in the pub as thirty-six year old Kevin Ritchie, an Elgin man who worked as a mechanic in a local garage. When questioned, he admitted that he had delivered a beige coloured 1984 Ford Fiesta car to Hector Dick at Wester Hillside Farm at Mosstowie just outside Elgin on 27th April, the day before Arlene disappeared. He also told the police that Nat Fraser had been present when he delivered the car and that Hector Dick paid him four hundred pounds in cash and gave him an extra fifty pounds in addition to the agreed price in exchange for him agreeing to keep his mouth shut. When the police interviewed Hector Dick, he absolutely denied ever owning a Ford Fiesta and said that he had never bought a car from Kevin Ritchie.

1984 Ford Fiesta similar to the one that Kevin Ritchie claimed he had sold to Hector Dick

Photo: Charlie

A short time later, the police talked to twenty-six year old Richard Murray, the manager of Spey Bay Salvage, a scrap yard located in the town of Fochabers, around ten miles from Elgin. He told them that in May 1998, three men had brought a partially-crushed beige Ford Fiesta to the yard. The car had subsequently been crushed and re-cycled.

Police questioned Hector Dick on over eighty occasions in 1999 about the Ford Fiesta and its disposal, but he continued to vehemently deny knowing anything about it. Finally, the police persuaded Kevin Ritchie to talk to Hector Dick about the car while wearing a recording device and in a location where the meeting could be filmed. Ritchie agreed and at the meeting Hector Dick was recorded talking about the Ford Fiesta and agreeing that he had bought it from Ritchie. Dick also gave Ritchie advice on what to do if he was questioned by the police:

> *"Just say you do not remember. You can only be charged with what you are caught with or what you say. Just turn your back and walk away from the bastards, just say nothing."*

This was advice which Hector Dick would follow himself for the next fifteen years. In October 1999 both Hector Dick and Nat Fraser were charged with perverting the course of justice with regard to the Ford Fiesta. Both denied the charges and both were due to appear in court in Elgin. The charge against Nat Fraser was later dropped and Hector Dick's defence team lodged an appeal that he was unlikely to receive a fair and unbiased hearing in Elgin and requested that the trial be re-located. The trial was deferred.

While the police continued to investigate the Fiesta, Nat Fraser found himself in court. Not as a result of his wife's disappearance, but as a result of the attempted murder charge that was raised against him in March 1998 following his Mother's Day attack on Arlene. On 1st March 2000, Fraser appeared in the High Court in Edinburgh to receive his sentence. Following some complex behind-the-scenes legal wrangling, the original attempted murder charge had been reduced to *"assault to the danger of life"*. Arlene's family, who all believed that Nat was involved in her disappearance, were naturally disappointed by the lesser charge but Nat Fraser lodged a plea of guilty and was sentenced to eighteen months in prison for what the judge, Lord Morison, called a *"nasty, wholly unprovoked and dangerous assault"*.

Nat Fraser was released from prison in December 2000 and Hector Dick finally appeared in court in Dingwall in February 2001 on a charge of perverting the course of justice over his lies about the Ford Fiesta. He lodged a plea of Not Guilty and for the first four days of the trial absolutely denied knowing anything about the Fiesta. However, on the fifth day of the trial he abruptly changed his plea to Guilty after Sheriff James Fraser ruled that video footage of Dick discussing the car with Kevin Ritchie was admissible as evidence. Dick claimed that his previous denials to police were due to the car being used as part of the drink smuggling operation that he and Nat Fraser had been running and not because it had been involved in Arlene's disappearance. Hector Dick was sentenced to one year in prison.

The Grampian Police team investigating Arlene's disappearance continued to believe that the missing car had been used as part of the plot to abduct Arlene. This was never proven. All that the saga of the Fiesta demonstrated for certain was that Hector Dick was very willing to lie, both to the police and in court, under oath. Hector Dick served his time in Porterfield prison in Inverness.

During his incarceration, Hector Dick was subject to further, intense questioning by the police about Arlene's disappearance. On June 21st he attempted to commit suicide by hanging himself. The attempt was unsuccessful and he later explained that he had been *"on a downward spiral"* at the time.

Part of the reason for his depression may have been the knowledge that Nat Fraser was back in prison, also in Porterfield, and he seemed to have lost faith in his former friend. In April 2001, Nat Fraser was found guilty of fraudulently claiming £18,000 of legal aid during his previous assault trial. It was discovered that Fraser had substantial savings which he had concealed from the authorities in order to qualify for legal aid. The Sheriff, James Penman, told Fraser that this was a very serious crime and that there was no alternative but to impose a custodial sentence. Just four months after being released from prison following the assault charge, Nat Fraser was sentenced to another twelve months behind bars.

During Nat Fraser's first period of incarceration on the

assault charge, there occurred what the police claimed was one of the most significant events of the investigation. Nat Fraser was visited in prison by Glenn Lucas, a man who ran his own fruit and vegetable business in Spalding in Lincolnshire. Lucas had been a childhood friend of Nat Fraser and had helped him set up his fruit and vegetable partnership with Ian Taylor. Lucas was known to Grampian Police because he had made a number of complaints about the police handling of the Arlene Fraser investigation, claiming that his friend was being unfairly treated.

Grampian Police were interested in anyone who was visiting Nat Fraser in prison, so they asked to view the relevant surveillance tapes. There were several visits by Glenn Lucas and, during one of them on 27th July 2000, police noted that the two men became involved in an obviously intense and heated discussion. There was just one problem – the tapes provided by the prison contained no sound. To assist them, the police contacted Jessica Rees, one of the UK's leading professional forensic lip readers.

Ms Rees had been profoundly deaf from birth and had obtained a degree from Balliol College, Oxford before she became a professional forensic lip reader in 1995. Forensic lip reading is extremely difficult because it involves lip-reading from media, usually from CCTV or video tapes. Image quality is often poor and the subject is rarely facing directly towards the camera. By 2000 Jessica Rees had built up an enviable reputation for being able to produce results even in the most difficult circumstances —she had provided her services in hundreds of cases, assisting both the police and legal representatives. She had testified in cases that resulted in the conviction of members of the IRA, the Russian Mafia and cheating lawyers.

Grampian Police asked her to view and provide a transcript for the conversation between Glenn Lucas and Nat Fraser. In cases where a forensic lip reader is being asked to provide an interpretation which may be used in court, the police are not supposed to provide any clue or context about why they want this conversation interpreted or what they expected it to cover. When Grampian Police sent the tapes to Ms Rees, they also sent a case summary. Fortunately, this was clearly marked and Ms Rees said that she had it sealed up and placed in a locked filing cabinet before she undertook the attempt to produce a transcript from the tapes.

Within a few weeks, Ms Rees provided a report to Grampian Police. This was explosive. Part of her transcription of what Nat Fraser had said included: *"Her arms are off and I pulled her teeth out. They can't find her. It's impossible isn't it?"* Later in the conversation she reported that he said: "I'll get away with it. It's all right. There's no evidence. It's *all down the plughole, so the police don't know shite. So fuck the lot of 'em!"* She also noted that more than once during the conversation Nat Fraser mentioned that he was concerned that someone called '*Hecky*' (presumably Hector Dick) might crack under pressure and tell the police something that he shouldn't and that he was worried that the police might find bank cards that he had hidden.

The investigating officers were exultant. Here at last was evidence directly linking Nat Fraser to Arlene's murder. The context and circumstances of the conversation also strongly suggested that both Glenn Lucas and Hector Dick had been involved. If they could be confident about Ms Rees interpretation, they had a good basis for proceeding with charges against all three men. Jessica Rees assured them that her transcript was completely reliable. *"I have to be very confident indeed to include any words in the transcript. And this only happens after an exhaustive process, which involves looking at sections of tape 40, 50, 60 times."*

In October 2001, Nat Fraser was released from prison in Inverness after serving just over six months for the legal aid fraud charge. He tried to pick up the threads of his life, but he was constantly being questioned by the police about Arlene's disappearance. He was no longer on first name terms with the investigating officers. It was now clear that the police team regarded this as a murder investigation and that Nat Fraser was their main suspect.

Unknown to Nat Fraser, the police also had one other very significant piece of circumstantial evidence. On the 29th April, the day after Arlene's disappearance, police had carried out a detailed search of the bungalow on Smith Street. This had included the production of a video showing the condition of all the rooms in the house. After Arlene's disappearance, her step mother, Catherine McInnes, began to pop in to look after the house. She had visited on several occasions when she went back on the afternoon of 7th May 1998, eight days after Arlene was last seen. To her surprise, when she went to clean the bathroom, Mrs McInnis found three rings hanging on a wooden dowel under the soap dish. These turned out to be Arlene's engagement, wedding and eternity rings and Mrs McInnis was certain that they hadn't been there when she had previously visited the house.

Police officers reviewed the video they had made in the house on 29th April. This showed the bathroom and it was clear that there were no rings on the wooden dowel at that time, confirming what Mrs McInnis had told them. Sometime between the 29th April and 7th May, someone had returned the rings to the house and placed them where Arlene Fraser normally kept them when she wasn't wearing them.

The injunction that prevented Nat Fraser from visiting the house had been lifted as of 7th May. So, the only people that had access to the house during that period were Mrs McInnis, Grampian Police and Nat Fraser. If Mrs McInnis and Grampian Police didn't place them there, that left only one possibility: that Arlene had been wearing her rings when she was abducted and murdered and that Nat Fraser had returned them to the house as soon as he was able.

On April 26th 2002, the Crown Office announced that Nat Fraser, Hector Dick and Glenn Lucas had been charged with murder, conspiracy to murder and attempting to defeat the ends of justice. Only Nat Fraser had an obvious motive for the crime and Hector Dick was included mainly because of his lies about the Ford Fiesta. The charge against Glenn Lucas was raised solely on the basis of the transcript of his discussion with Nat Fraser in prison. The police weren't certain what his role in the abduction and murder had been, but they knew that he had been in Elgin a few days before Arlene disappeared and were confident that he was implicated somehow.

Chapter 7: In court

January 2003

On Tuesday, January 7th 2003, the trial of the three men began in Court Number 3 at the High Court in Edinburgh before Lord McKay of Drumadoon. Nat Fraser was so confident of his acquittal that he had approached several tabloid newspapers beforehand, offering to sell his story for £80,000 after the trial. It was, he told them, the story of an innocent man unfairly hounded by the police for a crime he did not commit.

For the first four days of the trial, the jury listened as the prosecution set out what they believed to be the course of events. On Friday 10th January the court was shown the video showing that Arlene's rings were not in the bathroom on 29th April and then heard testimony from Catherine McInnes of how they had re-appeared by the time she went to the house on 7th May. The trial was then adjourned for the weekend.

When it re-started on Tuesday 14th January, most people expected more of the same. Instead, the Crown Office made a dramatic announcement: they would not be continuing with any of the charges against either Hector Dick or Glenn Lucas. Both men were released unconditionally. However, prosecution Advocate depute Alan Turnbull QC explained that the prosecution now intended to call Hector Dick as a witness against Nat Fraser.

Hector Dick had, it transpired, made a very favourable deal during the weekend. In addition to the charges against him in this case, he was also being pursued by HM Revenue and Customs for unpaid revenue arising from the smuggled booze racket. He was facing a ruinous revenue bill of £250,000, something he could have paid only by selling his farm.

Hector Dick agreed that he would that he would provide testimony against Nat Fraser in exchange for the dropping of the murder charge against him and for the dropping of all charges by HMRC. This was agreed and a *"letter of comfort"* was produced by HMRC confirming that they would not pursue Dick for unpaid revenue. The decision to drop the charges against Glenn Lucas seems to have been based solely on a lack of evidence (other than the transcripts made by Jessica Rees, and it was not intended that these should be produced in court) rather than any deals made and Lucas was not called to give evidence at the trial. The charges against Nat Fraser were modified to claim that he had arranged the abduction and murder of Arlene with *"unknown accomplices"*.

The judge adjourned the trial to allow the defence team

time to interview Hector Dick. The trial re-convened on Monday 20th January. For the first two days, most of the testimony was given by Hector Dick. He now provided a very different account of events in April 1998. It was also notable that he did not once look at Nat Fraser as he spoke and that, for the first time, the accused man looked nervous and apprehensive in the dock.

Dick was asked about his role in procuring the beige Ford Fiesta which had been of such interest to the police. He had claimed at his 2001 trial for perverting the course of justice that the car had been purchased for use in the drink smuggling operation in which he and Nat Fraser were involved. Now, he told the court that the car had been purchased at the request of Nat Fraser and left in the yard of his farm with the keys in it on the evening of 27th April. At some point that night it was removed, though he did not see who took it. On Sunday 3rd May, the car reappeared, with a bundle of children's clothing and a woman's brown coat in it. Dick then said that he had burned the car before crushing it as far as possible with the digger on his tractor before loading the wreck onto a trailer and taking it to the scrap yard in Elgin. This version of events was at least partly confirmed when Richard Murray, the manager of Spey Bay Salvage, testified that Hector Dick was one of the three men who had brought the Fiesta to his yard to be crushed in early May 1998.

Hector Dick's farm was in Mosstowie, just outside the town of Elgin and around a ten minute drive from Smith Street

Photo: Anne Burgess

Referring to the destruction of the car, Paul McBride QC, Nat Fraser's solicitor asked Dick:

> *"What kind of man takes it upon himself to destroy the evidence and her clothes and the clothes of her children when she is still missing and her family are still grieving. What kind of man does that, Mr Dick?"*
>
> Dick replied: *"I am not expecting no prizes."*

Hector Dick also spoke at length about his friendship with Nat Fraser. He claimed that, in the period between Fraser being ejected from the house in Smith Street after his attack on Arlene and before her disappearance, Nat Fraser had said several things that "*concerned*" Dick. Nat told him that more than 10,000 people went missing every year and were never found. He also said that Nat Fraser had gone to Elgin library and looked through reference books. He then told Dick that only two people in Scotland had ever been convicted of murder when a body could not be found and that forensic scientists needed at least three inches of bone to make a positive identification. He also said, Dick claimed, that he knew people *"who did things like that"*.

Dick told the court that Nat Fraser was very jealous of his wife, worried that she might be seeing other men and that he could not bear the thought of his children living with another man. He was also terrified that Arlene might pursue a divorce settlement that could cost him up to £86,000.

When he was asked how he felt when he heard that Arlene had disappeared, Hector Dick said that he had been "*alarmed*". Paul McBride pointed out correctly that most of what Hector Dick had previously told police and said at his trial in 2001 was untrue. He described Dick as a *"habitual, serial liar"*. Dick admitted lying, but claimed that was because "*my loyalty was to Nat at that time.*"

McBride described some parts of Hector Dick's testimony as "*preposterous, unbelievable and a pack of lies*". He went on to ask Hector Dick several awkward questions:

> McBride: "*Why did you not tell the police the truth (about the Ford Fiesta)?*
>
> Hector Dick: "*I was already trapped.*"
>
> McBride: "*How many lies have you told to the authorities in the last five years?*"
>
> Hector Dick: "*Quite a few.*"
>
> McBride: "*You have had plenty of practice.*"
>
> Hector Dick: "*I have had a bit, yes.*"
>
> McBride: "*More than a bit, you are a practised, consummate and habitual liar.*"

Finally, on Friday 24th January, Nat Fraser was called to give evidence. He told the court that he loved Arlene though he admitted that their marriage was "*quite stormy at times*". For legal reasons the jury were not told of Fraser's previous conviction for the Mother's Day assault on Arlene. Nat Fraser categorically denied murdering Arlene or being involved in any way in her abduction or murder. Alan Turnbull QC for the prosecution put the case succinctly:

> Turnbull : *"Arlene had no enemies and the only person she had any trouble with in her life was you. When you take all of that together it is perfectly clear, isn't it, you are the only person with any advantage to gain from the death of your wife?"*
>
> Fraser: *"I didn't kill my wife. I didn't."*
>
> Turnbull: *"It is clear you were the only person with any advantage to gain from the death of your wife, isn't it?"*
>
> Fraser: *"Looks like it, yes."*

That was the core of the prosecution case. The extensive police *"presumption of death"* investigation made it virtually certain that Arlene Fraser was dead. No-one other than Nat Fraser had any known reason to kill her. The testimony of Hector Dick seemed to suggest strongly that Nat Fraser had arranged the murder of his wife, though the fact that Dick was known to have previously lied under oath must have raised questions about his veracity. The only hard evidence was that of the rings. The rings weren't there on April 29th when Grampian Police made their video. They were there on 7th May when they were discovered by Mrs

McInnis. They could only have been placed there by Mrs McInnis, Grampian Police or Nat Fraser. Grampian Police and Mrs McInnis were adamant that they had not put the rings there. That left Nat Fraser, who had access to the house from the morning of 7th May. The rings became the most important single piece of evidence against Nat Fraser. In his closing address for the prosecution on 28th January, Alan Turnbull held up the rings, one by one while he spoke to the jury:

> *"The discovery of these rings represents one of the most compelling pieces of evidence that you will ever hear in a court in a case of this kind. These rings tell us that the dead body of Arlene Fraser was available eight or nine days after her disappearance. These are the rings he gave to his young wife, the mother of his children. How ironic these tokens of love, permanence and fidelity should end up being his undoing. There is something inherently just in the way that, after death, something of Arlene's can reach back and ensnare the man who promised he would live with her for ever then took her life just because it no longer suited his purposes."*

In his summing-up the judge, Lord Mackay, told the jury that that they could only convict Nat Fraser of murder if they accepted that it was him who had placed the rings in the bathroom in Smith Street on May 7th.

On 29th January 2003 the jury returned with a majority verdict: *"Guilty"*. Nat Fraser blinked rapidly, slumped in his seat and then stared fixedly at the floor. There were shouts of *"Yes!"* from members of Arlene's family. In pronouncing sentence, Lord McKay called Fraser *"evil"* and told him *"someone will have to explain to your two children that you have now been convicted of killing their mother - you, the father who has looked after those two children since their mother's death"*. Nat Fraser was sentenced to life imprisonment with a recommendation that he serve a minimum of twenty-five years. As the sentence was read out he seemed to collapse and had to be assisted to leave the court as he was led away a short time later.

Chapter 8: Doubts

February 2003 – April 2005

As far as most people were concerned, that was the end of the story. Thanks in part to some smart police work in identifying the significance of the missing rings in the video, a murderer had been sent to prison. After Nat Fraser's conviction, Grampian Police also revealed to the press how the information provided by Jessica Rees had helped convince them of his guilt (the transcript of the conversation between Nat Fraser and Glenn Lucas had not been introduced at the trial). They vowed to continue to try to find Arlene's body.

On 21st April 2003 a memorial service was held for Arlene in Elgin. Friends and family, recognising that there would most likely never be a funeral, held the service to remember her almost five years after her disappearance.

In the Queen's Birthday Honours list issued on 13th June 2003, Detective Superintendent Jim Stephen of Grampian Police received the Queen's Police Medal for his work on the Arlene Fraser case.

Other events which followed the end of the trial were less edifying. On 31st January 2003, the first of a series of articles about the Arlene Fraser case had appeared in the Daily Record newspaper. These purported to be based on exclusive revelations provided by Hector Dick to the newspaper. It seems that, on the weekend of 11/12th January, Dick hadn't just been negotiating with the Crown Office to have the charges against him dropped, he was also negotiating a lucrative deal with the Daily Record to provide them with exclusive details of the case – it is said that he received a payment of £20,000 for his story.

In these articles Hector Dick made a series of new statements about the case which differed significantly to the evidence he had given in court. Amongst other things he claimed that Nat Fraser had hired a professional killer from "*down south*" who had gone to the house in Smith Street on 28th April and strangled Arlene. Nat Fraser had then gone to the house, removed the body, cleaned up the scene and finally burned Arlene's body on a barbecue in a charcoal pit in woodland close to Elgin. Many people were left wondering how someone who was, by his own admission, an accessory to murder could be allowed to sell his story to a newspaper? Arlene's family complained to the Press Complaints Commission about this series of articles but their complaints were not upheld. Hector Dick went on to provide "*exclusives*" to the Daily Record on the Arlene Fraser case on several subsequent occasions.

In December 2003 Glenn Lucas, who claimed to be completely disgusted with continuing insinuations that he had been involved in Arlene's disappearance, persuaded the News of the World newspaper to pay for and witness him undertaking a lie detector test to refute these allegations. The test was carried out in Lucas' home in Spalding and was administered by Bruce Burgess, one of the UK's leading polygraph operators. Burgess worked regularly for banks and other financial institutions, administering lie detector tests to staff as well as testing on behalf of popular television shows including Trisha and the Channel 4 breakfast show RI:SE. Burgess asked Glenn Lucas a number of questions of which the most significant were:

> *Were you in any way involved in killing of Arlene Fraser?* Lucas answered *"No".*

> *To your certain knowledge was Nat Fraser involved in the killing of his wife Arlene?* Lucas answered *"No".*

> *Do you know where Arlene is now?* Lucas answered *"No".*

Burgess reported that in each case, Glenn Lucas was telling the truth. Lucas was delighted, telling the News of the World:

> *"I hope that the people who still whisper when they see me will now accept I am innocent. What more can you do to clear your name than put yourself through a test like this?"*

This wasn't Glenn Lucas' only involvement n the case. In April 2005 a book about the case, *Murdered or Missing?: The Arlene Fraser Case* was published. The book was written by professional crime writer Reg McKay who had previously published several books about sensational Scottish crime cases. The co-author was Glenn Lucas. The book, which was also serialized in a Scottish tabloid, claimed to be a true account of the case though in reality it was mostly an attempt by Lucas to exonerate his friend. It did this by proposing two equally implausible but also completely contradictory scenarios.

First, it suggested that Arlene Fraser wasn't dead at all and that instead she had walked out on her life and her children on 28th April to pursue a new existence elsewhere. The main basis for this seemed to be that there had been a few alleged sightings of Arlene after she was supposed to have died. These weren't at all convincing – one was a sighting of a woman who was said to look like Arlene on a beach in Northern Cyprus. This scenario didn't really stand up to close examination – developing an entirely new identity, which is what Arlene would have been required to do if she was still alive, is extremely difficult and requires time, a great deal of money and access to criminals who have some very specialized skills. The book didn't even attempt to explain how she did this, though it did quote one witness who said that Arlene had shown her a false passport. This wasn't widely believed and to base a whole theory on nothing more than a couple of supposed sightings is a very long stretch indeed.

The book seemed to accept this because it also claimed that, if Arlene had actually been murdered, then the killer was not necessarily Nat Fraser. It discussed at length what it called the *"corrupt underbelly of life in her small community"*. This revolved round Arlene's supposed drink and drug habit, her alleged affairs and the illicit drink smuggling racket that was operating in Elgin. It suggested (without producing any hard evidence to back up this contention) that Arlene was somehow directly involved in the smuggling racket and might have been killed by members of the gang from Fife because of this.

The book also attacked and ridiculed the testimony of Hector Dick. This wasn't especially difficult – Dick was a known liar and his account of what had happened had changed so often that even he must have found it difficult to remember what he had said at any given time. The book did raise one particular point that seemed to directly undermine Dick's testimony at the trial. Despite police claiming initially that the Ford Fiesta had been dumped at a scrap yard in Fochabers, at the trial Dick had described in detail how he had taken both the partly crushed car and an unwanted stainless steel tank from his farm to a scrapyard in Elgin. When the owner of that yard was contacted, he was adamant that the car had never been taken there and he was able to produce a receipt for the stainless steel tank which Dick claimed to have dropped off at the same time – the receipt showed that the tank had been dropped off by Dick in 1996, more than two years before Arlene disappeared. If Dick had lied about this, the book argued, why should we accept any of his other testimony?

The book also spent time suggesting that Arlene was not the respectable housewife that most people took her for. A witness was found who claimed to have seen Arlene at drug parties in nearby Banff and Cullen and it was said that she consumed large amounts of alcohol, especially vodka procured by Nat as part of the smuggling racket. Most of her friends were outraged and angry at these suggestions. She was, they pointed out, a devoted mother who spent her evenings with the children except for the occasional Saturday night when she went out with her friends. They also pointed out that her Crohn's disease meant that she was never able to have more than a couple of drinks and she certainly could not have been taking drugs.

The one possibility that the book didn't spend any time on was that Nat Fraser might have been directly involved in Arlene's disappearance though it did raise some interesting questions about the Grampian Police investigation. It claimed, for example, that Grampian Police had decided from the outset that Nat Fraser had murdered his wife and stated that key witnesses were bullied by police to ensure that they produced testimony which supported this view.

It was certainly notable that some witnesses had changed their evidence in ways that tended to support the police version of events. For example, when Richard Murray, the manager of Spey Bay Salvage was first interviewed in October 1998 about the men who brought the beige Ford Fiesta to the yard, he described the man he had spoken to as being *"in his early twenties"*. Surprisingly, in late 2002 and after Hector Dick, Nat Fraser and Glenn Lucas had been charged with Arlene's murder, he positively identified 45 year old Hector Dick as being the man he had spoken to.

Hazel Walker, the young woman Nat Fraser had called during the morning of 28th April, claimed that she was subject to such intense harassment by officers from Grampian Police that she attempted suicide by taking an overdose of paracetamol.

There were several other instances where witnesses seemed to have modified their statements of what had happened to accord more closely with the police version of events, with Hector Dick being the most notable example. Individually these amounted to little, but collectively some people began to see them as evidence that Grampian Police had put pressure on witnesses to support the story they wanted the court to hear.

The most damaging attack on the police case which was raised in the book and discussed elsewhere involved Arlene's rings. The contention that only Nat Fraser could have left them in the bungalow on Smith Street had been central to the prosecution case at the murder trial, but doubts were beginning to arise over the version of events given in court.

The main problem was that the two police officers who had visited the bungalow on the evening of the 28th April were both adamant that they had seen the rings in the bathroom on that occasion. Constable Julie Clark said of her visit on that evening:

> *"The one thing which has stuck in my mind was I noticed jewellery. As far as I can recollect there were three rings and a yellow metal bracelet or necklace, a chain. I thought it unusual for a woman to leave home without what appeared to me to be a wedding ring, an engagement ring and an eternity ring."*

Her colleague PC Neil Lynch who accompanied her on the visit also recalled seeing jewelry on a shelf by the bathroom sink. He claimed that he had pointed this out to a Crown official in 2002, before the trial. The Crown official who took the statement had realised the importance of what Lynch had told him and left a note with a draft copy of the statement on the desk of the then Procurator Fiscal for Elgin, David Dickson. David Dickerson denied ever having seen this note and was unable to provide an explanation when a copy was later found in the Procurator's case file.

This was vital information. Nat Fraser's conviction for murder depended partly on the fact that only he could have replaced the rings there, which in turn meant that he must have had access to Arlene's body. The new version of events suggested very strongly that the rings must have been removed on the 29th April (and subsequently replaced) by someone from Grampian Police.

It was claimed that the rings missing from the Fraser bungalow were seen in the desk of a Detective Sergeant from Grampian Police. The claim was made by PC David Alexander, who was initially part of the Arlene Fraser investigation. Constable Alexander appeared in court on a Breach if the Peace charge in 2004, which led to his suspension from Grampian Police. During the trial he mentioned "*irregularities*" and a "*cover-up*" in the Arlene Fraser investigation. He was later persuaded by Nat Fraser's legal team to make a sworn statement in front of a Sheriff in which he noted that he hadn't seen the rings himself, but claimed that he was told about them by Detective Sergeant David Slessor, another officer involved in the case. Thirty-three year old Slessor was found dead in his home in Aberdeen in July 1998 after he had apparently committed suicide.

This was explosive stuff. It suggested very strongly that some members of Grampian Police had deliberately withheld information that might have changed the outcome of a murder trial. Nat Fraser's lawyers lodged an appeal against his conviction.

Chapter 9: A free man

May 2005 – April 2010

Suddenly, Nat Fraser's conviction looked much less secure. In early May 2005, he was given leave to appeal against the verdict of the murder trial. In March 2006, an investigation was announced into the police handling of the Arlene Fraser investigation. Officers from Strathclyde Police were to carry out a review of the way in which the investigation had been carried out and particularly to look at the question of the rings. As more information emerged throughout the early part of 2006, pressure increased on the Crown Office. On 12th May 2006 they took an unprecedented step: Nat Fraser was freed on bail pending the result of his appeal against his murder conviction.

Julie Clark and Neil Lynch, the Grampian Police officers who claimed to have seen the rings on 28th April, were both questioned at length and both claimed that they had been subjected to pressure to change their stories when the importance of the rings became apparent. During an interview with the then Procurator Fiscal for Elgin, Sharon Ralph, in 2006, Julie Clark broke down. She told the Procurator that she felt that her police career was over and that she would be branded a "*grass*" for speaking out about the rings. She also claimed that she had been told to say nothing about what she had seen by other police officers. Constable Neil Lynch was interviewed by Detective Constable Andrew Wright of Strathclyde Police during 2006. Lynch claimed that at that interview he was put under extreme pressure to change his statement and admit that he had not seen the rings. He refused and said that as a result, his career in Grampian Police was effectively over. He resigned soon after.

The investigation into Grampian Police continued throughout 2006, but in September there was a blow for Nat and his supporters: Glenn Lucas died of a heart-attack in his home in Lincolnshire aged just 55. Within days, Hector Dick emerged from the obscurity his pig farm and provided the Daily Record with another exclusive, this time an attack on Lucas.

Hector Dick told the newspaper that Lucas had known more about Arlene's disappearance than he ever admitted (it may or may not be relevant to note here that a charge of libel cannot be raised on behalf of a dead person). He also told how Glenn Lucas had come to his farm in 2005 and had threatened his life if he said anything else that might harm Nat Fraser. He claimed that, as part of their investigation into the case, officers from Strathclyde Police had come to his farm in early 2006 to warn him they were aware of a *"credible threat"* that his life might be in danger. The Daily Record was able to confirm that Strathclyde Police took the threat so seriously that they issued an *"Osman Notice"* to Dick, something that is only done when police believe that there is a real danger to the life of a specified target. Dick claimed that they refused to tell him whether Glenn Lucas was the source but, ten days after Glenn Lucas died, officers returned to his farm to tell him that the threat to his life had diminished.

Hector Dick

Photo: The Northern Scot

On Tuesday 13th November 2007, Nat Fraser, still free on bail and confident that his murder conviction would soon be overturned, attended the start of his appeal hearing at the High Court in Edinburgh before Lord Johnstone. The defence case was simple – the police evidence concerning the rings had been a central part of the prosecution case in the original trial. It was now clear that this evidence was seriously flawed – at the beginning of the appeal, Nat Fraser's QC, Peter Gray was asked by Lord Johnstone whether he thought this was due to an error or a deliberate attempt to influence the trial? His careful response was:

> *"Not a cover up. I don't suggest this was a cover up but there was an extraordinary degree of incompetence."*

The prosecution case was equally simple: despite the fact that at the previous trial the rings had been described as the "*cornerstone*" of the prosecution case, it was now said that there had been ample other evidence to convict Nat Fraser even without the evidence of the rings. John Beckett QC, acting for the Crown, told the court:

> *"It remains the case that there was and is a compelling body of circumstantial evidence giving*

> *rise to an almost irresistible inference that the appellant was, as the jury determined, guilty of being involved in the instigation of the murder of his wife, the deceased Arlene Fraser."*

The appeal went back and forth for more than two weeks before all the evidence had finally been heard. Then, to the amazement of almost everyone involved, Lord Johnstone ordered that Nat Fraser should go back to prison while awaiting the outcome of the appeal, even though this might take several months. In the event, it took six more months, until 8th May 2008 and after the tenth anniversary of Arlene's disappearance before the verdict was announced: the appeal was refused and the verdict stood. Nat Fraser was to remain in prison and serve out the remainder of his sentence.

This was a completely unexpected blow for Nat Fraser and his few remaining supporters and in October 2008 Fraser's legal team asked judges at the Court of Criminal Appeal for leave to appeal to the Privy Council in London? This was refused in March 2009. In November 2009, Fraser claimed at the Court of Criminal Appeal in Edinburgh that he did not get a fair hearing at his appeal. This was refused and judged incompetent. In early 2010, Nat Fraser announced that he would appeal his case at the Supreme Court in London.

The hearing began in London on 21st March 2010. On 25th March the result was announced: Nat Fraser's appeal was upheld and his conviction for the murder of his wife was quashed. Nat Fraser was once again a free man.

Lord Hope, one of the Supreme Court appeal judges, provided a written account of the reasoning behind the decision:

> *"The fact is that the Crown chose to present the case at the trial in a way that it would not have chosen to do if it had been aware at the time of the trial that there was evidence that the rings were in the house within hours of Arlene's disappearance....it was information that ought to have been given to the defence, and the failure to do this was a breach of the appellant's right to a fair trial".*

The Crown Office immediately announced that it would be seeking to bring fresh murder proceedings against Nat Fraser. Arlene Fraser's family, understandably horrified and confused said that: *"Today's decision by the Supreme Court is bitterly disappointing. We accept today's decision. However, we fully support the Crown's intention to seek authority to bring fresh proceedings against Nat Fraser for Arlene's murder."*

Many people were very confused indeed about the prospect of a second trial: what about double jeopardy? This is a legal precept which states that a person should not be tried twice for the same crime. However, there is a caveat: the concept of double jeopardy is based on the notion that a person cannot be tried again for the same crime once they have been to court *and received a valid conviction or acquittal*. The fact that the Supreme Court in London had quashed Nat Fraser's guilty verdict meant that technically, he hadn't received a valid conviction. Thus, he could be tried again.

That didn't make it fair – there could hardly have been a person in Scotland who hadn't heard about Nat Fraser and his previous conviction so the chances of finding members of a jury who would be unbiased was approximately zero. But then, the legal system is based on a requirement for justice, not on a guarantee of fairness.

Chapter 10: Read my lips

May 2010 - March 2012

It was recognised that it would take time for a new murder trial to be organised and, for the next two years, Nat Fraser remained free on bail. Life can't have been easy for him back in Elgin. By this time there was a widespread acceptance that he probably had instigated Arlene's murder and one can imagine that a chance meeting between, for example, Nat Fraser and Hector Dick would have been very awkward indeed.

In addition to frantic legal manoeuvring, there were other significant developments in this period. One concerned Jessica Rees, the lip reader who had provided Grampian Police with a damning transcript that seemed to show Nat Fraser discussing the disposal of Arlene's body with Glenn Lucas in Porterfield prison. After the first murder trial, Grampian Police had released this information to the press, noting that it was this transcript that had finally persuaded them to charge Nat Fraser with murder.

The release of extracts from these transcripts certainly had the desired effect. Before the trial, there were many people in the Elgin area who believed in Nat Fraser's innocence.

Even after his conviction, some remained. After the transcripts were released in which he appeared to be discussing cutting off his wife's arms and pulling out her teeth, a wave of revulsion swept the area. It would have been easier to find a unicorn in Elgin than a person who believed in Nat Fraser's innocence. Fraser's business partner Ian Taylor was typical. Before the trial, he was totally supportive of Nat Fraser and proclaimed his partner's innocence to anyone who would listen. After the verdict and the revelation of the transcripts, he issued a statement noting that he had been misled and that he wanted nothing further to do with Nat Fraser. He changed the name of the fruit and vegetable business from '*Taylor and Fraser*' to '*Speyfruit*' and later sued his ex-partner for £20,000 over an unpaid tax bill.

In 2005, the Crown Prosecution Service in England issued a notice that it would not be using Jessica Rees as an expert witness in current or future cases. The notice went on to say:

> *"As a precaution, the Crown Prosecution Service is contacting defendants or their representatives in those cases where Jessica Rees gave evidence for the prosecution and which resulted in a conviction. They will be provided with a disclosure package to enable them to advise their clients."*

Part of the problem was that, in 2005, Ms Rees had been giving testimony as an expert witness at a case in Snaresbrook Crown Court in London. A diligent defence barrister, Edward Henry, who had carefully done his homework pointed out that Ms Rees did not actually have a degree from Oxford as she claimed. This alone was enough for the CPS to decide not to use her again as an expert witness, but worse was to follow. By the time that Nat Fraser was waiting for his second trial to begin, some of the work that Ms Rees had done as an expert witness had been reviewed, and the findings were very worrying.

Professor Summerfield of the Medical Research Council Institute of Hearing Research in Nottingham for example, was asked to test Jessica Rees's lip-reading skills. In a test involving 820 words, Professor Summerfield noted that she got fifty-five per cent correct, which isn't actually a bad score for a lip-reader. More worryingly, he also reported that she identified 224 words that were not spoken.

Other, experienced forensic lip readers were asked to review a video tape from which Ms Rees had produced a 2,100 word transcript in 1999. They agreed with only 234 of the words provided by Ms Rees. Experts reviewed her findings in other cases and said that some of the video tapes from which she had worked were simply of too poor quality to allow <u>any</u> lip reading to be done. Yet somehow, Jessica Rees had provided detailed transcripts based on these tapes.

The tapes of Nat Fraser's conversation in Porterfield prison were shown to Terry Ruane, a well respected and experienced forensic lip reader and the owner of Theatresign, a company which provides sign language interpreters for live performances. After a detailed study, Mr Ruane admitted that he was unable to agree with <u>any</u> of the key words provided by Ms Rees in her transcript. It was clear that there were, at the very least, serious doubts over Ms Rees transcripts of Nat Fraser's conversation with Glenn Lucas, particularly when it became clear that she had been in contact with Arlene's family, though it was not known whether this happened before or after she produced the transcript.

Probably unsurprisingly, the concerns about the reliability of Jessica Rees' work received much less press coverage than had the initial sensational reporting of her transcripts. Most people were left with a vague notion that Nat Fraser must be guilty because he had been recorded while talking about disposing of his wife's body.

Chapter 11: In court again

April 2012 – present

The second trial began on 23rd April 2012, almost exactly fourteen years after Arlene had disappeared. Nat Fraser was accused of instigating the murder of Arlene between April 28 and May 7, 1998 in Smith Street or elsewhere with the assistance of unknown accomplices. The trial was held in the High Court in Edinburgh before Lord Bracadale who imposed considerable restrictions on media reporting during the trial. The Judge opened by warning the jury that they must put out of their minds anything they thought they knew about the case and concentrate only on the testimony given before them. Nat Fraser lodged special defences of alibi and incrimination. The defence team claimed that Fraser had an alibi which meant that he could not have murdered Arlene and named Hector Dick as the actual murderer.

The High Court of of Justiciary, Edinburgh

Photo: LornaMCampbell

The early part of the trial highlighted further concerns about the Grampian Police handling of the case. For example, it was revealed that a forensic scientist, Neville Trower, had been called to the bungalow on 29th April. One of the things he was asked to do was to check both for signs of a struggle and to look for blood spatter which might not be visible to the naked eye by using luminal, a chemical that causes even tiny blood stains to glow when they are subjected to ultraviolet light. However, Trower did not have the required window black-out blinds with him when he went to the bungalow. He returned on 11th May with the appropriate equipment and carried out the test which did not reveal the presence of any blood spatter. Trower was surprised when he returned to discover that members of the Fraser family had been living in the house since Arlene's disappearance – normal procedure was for a suspected crime scene to sealed until all forensic testing was complete to ensure that evidence could not be removed by cleaning. The fact that the house had been lived in rendered further forensic examination virtually worthless.

Of course, no Nat Fraser murder trial would be complete without an appearance by Hector Dick and in this one, he played a starring role. Dick was the principle witness for the prosecution and for almost four interminable days he stumbled, rambled, repeated himself, contradicted himself and in response to many, many questions told the court that he simply couldn't remember.

The defence team raised several awkward questions for Dick. He was asked if he had not initially claimed that Nat Fraser had refused to tell him what he had done and only changed this when he was offered a deal by prosecutors and HMRC? He denied this but the defence produced an early statement he had given to the police in which he said: "*Nat has never told me what he's done but my opinion is he was involved in his wife's disappearance.*"

He was asked what he meant when he claimed to have crushed the Ford Fiesta and *"rolled it up like a carpet"*. He laughed and said that he would never have said this as it was not possible. It was pointed out that this was precisely what he had claimed at the first trial in 2003. The defence noted that Dick had claimed that Nat Fraser had shown him a website about getting rid of bodies before Arlene disappeared, but records proved that Fraser did not have an Internet connection at that time. Dick was unable to explain this.

The defence also referred to a letter from Dick's lawyer, sent to the Crown Office during negotiations before the start of the first trial, offering information and noting that the missing car was *"70% gettable"* and Arlene's body as *"40% gettable"*. Dick claimed that he had never said this and was unable to explain why his lawyer might have sent such a letter. He was also asked to explain what he meant when he had said *"the gullible bastards sitting there in the front bench will believe anything"* during the conversation with Kevin Ritchie secretly recorded by Grampian Police. He sheepishly admitted that he had been talking about juries in general. He claimed that the decision by HMRC not to prosecute him had played no part in persuading him to testify against Nat Fraser at the first trial. It was pointed out that he had absolutely refused to talk to police until he had the letter confirming that all charges were dropped.

Even without awkward questions from the defence, Hector Dick proved more than capable of tripping himself up. At one point in his testimony he told the court that his drink smuggling activities had been going on for around a year when Arlene disappeared, clearly forgetting that he had previously claimed that it had been no more than six weeks. He had previously said that he did not see either Nat Fraser or Kevin Ritchie on the night before Arlene disappeared, but in court he said that he had seen both. On one day of his testimony he claimed that he had paid £350 for the Fiesta. The following day he was certain it was £450. Seemingly just for a bit of variety, he suddenly claimed that Nat Fraser told him that gypsies had stolen the Ford Fiesta after it was used for the abduction of Arlene! He appeared to have forgotten the long, detailed story he had previously told the court about burning and crushing the car himself before taking it to the scrap yard. Dick was warned by the judge, once about perjury and once about prevarication and on one occasion was threatened with Contempt of Court for failing to answer questions.

The court also heard testimony from Hector Dick's brother, James, who had been working on the farm on the morning of 28th April 1998. James Dick told the court that "*I cannot remember seeing Hector at all that morning."* Hector had previously told the court that he had been working on the farm during the period when Arlene disappeared.

On 17th May, Ian *'Pedro'* Taylor was called to the stand. This was the first time that Taylor had been called to testify – he was not called as a witness at the first trial. Nat Fraser was staying with Taylor when Arlene disappeared. He was at Taylor's house when he received a call from Graham Higgins telling him that Arlene was missing. It was clear that the prosecution wanted Taylor to say that Nat Fraser might have left the house in Lhanbride on the evening of 28th April (presumably so that he could dispose of Arlene's body). Taylor did his best – he pointed out that he was a sound sleeper and that Nat's bedroom was at the front of the house, so he could have left without anyone noticing. None of this really mattered because it transpired that police had arrived at Taylor's house at 03:00 am that morning, looking for Fraser – he was there and spoke to them, apparently without his friend noticing. Taylor also told the court that Fraser had shown no emotion when he received the call, but he seemed confused when he was read back an earlier statement in which he had said that Fraser turned pale on hearing the news. He told the court that Fraser did not seem concerned about Arlene being missing, but he again appeared confused when he was reminded that he had originally told police the Fraser had suggested that the two of them should go round local hospitals to look for Arlene. He seemed even more confused when he was specifically asked if Nat Fraser had left his house that night? He gave the odd reply *"Was he in?"*

Ex-Constable Neil Lynch also gave evidence, telling the court that Arlene's rings had been there when he first visited the house on the evening of 28th April. He also told how he had come under continuing pressure, both from Grampian Police and from officers from Strathclyde Police who were investigating the case to change his story. The court also heard evidence from the manager and employees of the scrapyard where Hector Dick claimed to have dumped the Fiesta – all denied that he had done this.

One rather odd piece of evidence was heard from James Muirieson, a taxi driver from Elgin who had been living in a small caravan on Hector Dick's farm in April/May 1998. He claimed that, in response to a police appeal for information about the beige Fiesta, he contacted Grampian Police and told them that he had seen such a vehicle on Dick's farm on several occasions. He told the police that he had seen the car well into May, considerably after the date Dick claimed that he had got rid of it. Muirieson told the court that the police reacted very angrily to this, telling him that he was wrong and threatening him with prison and court if he persisted in claiming to have seen the Fiesta later in May.

Nat Fraser chose not to testify at this trial. A note was read out on his behalf stating that he had not consulted a library book about the lack of murder convictions in Scotland in cases where there was no body as Hector Dick had claimed. He had instead gone to the library to consult a book on family and child law in view of his separation from Arlene. This seemed a very trivial point when taken against the other very serious and damning allegations that Hector Dick had made.

On Monday 28th May, John Scott QC for the defence provided his closing address to the jury and noted that this was a "*difficult and anxious*" case, argued much of the Crown evidence was "*unreliable*" and that the original police investigation had been "*seriously flawed*". He might also have mentioned that the entire case was circumstantial and that the principal witness for the prosecution was a known liar who contradicted himself on several occasions. Perhaps he assumed that these things were so self-evident that they didn't need to be said?

On Tuesday 29th May, the eight women and seven men of the jury heard Lord Bracadale's directions, which included the unusual comment that they could still return a guilty verdict against Nat Fraser even if they rejected the evidence given by a key prosecution witness, a clear reference to Hector Dick's rambling, inconsistent and contradictory testimony. Perhaps the Judge wasn't convinced that the jury were as gullible as Hecky seemed to believe?

The jury were sent out to deliberate and the following day, 30th May 2012, they returned to court and announced that they had found Nat Fraser guilty of murder by majority verdict. Again. Nat Fraser looked shaken and stunned by the verdict. Again. Lord Bracadale told Fraser that he had arranged his wife's murder in cold blood and that his behaviour was both shocking and wicked. He sentenced him to serve at least seventeen years in prison without the possibility of parole. This made Fraser's potential release date 2029, the same as it had been when he was sentenced to twenty-five years after the first trial in 2003.

The second trial was filmed by cameras from Channel 4 and was broadcast on July 9th 2012 as *The Murder Trial*, a 90 minute documentary produced from edited highlights of the trial intercut with interviews with members of Arlene's family.

In July 2013 Hector Dick provided yet another exclusive to the Daily Record. He told the newspaper that Nat Fraser had attempted to have Arlene *"bumped off"* in Glasgow some time before her disappearance, but that she became suspicious and wouldn't take the trip. This came just one day after the same newspaper had carried a story originating from Nat Fraser's daughter Natalie where she said that she believed that Hector Dick was her mother's murderer.

In September 2013, Nat Fraser appealed the verdict of the second trial on the basis that a comment by a witness, Sandra Stewart, was prejudicial in that it mentioned his previous conviction for assault on Arlene. In theory, the jury were not supposed to know about this. The appeal was refused.

Nat Fraser continues to claim that he is innocent and has attempted to appeal the verdict of the second trial on a number of basis (for example, one juror was reportedly overheard on a bus saying that she believed Fraser to be guilty during the early stages of the trial), but none of these have been accepted to date. Nat Fraser will be eligible for parole in 2029 when he is sixty-nine years of age.

Arlene's family continue to believe that Nat Fraser is guilty of arranging her disappearance, though several of them are also convinced that Hector Dick was the actual murderer. Natalie is now married with her own children, though for a time she split from her husband and she and Jamie lived in the house in Smith Street.

Hector Dick continues to work his farm at Mosstowie near Elgin. It has now been several years since the Daily Record carried one of his exclusive stories.

Ian '*Pedro*' Taylor continues to operate his fruit and vegetable business in Elgin, though nowadays the day-to-day running of the business is done by younger members of the Taylor family. In May 2017 he stood as an independent candidate in council elections in the Fochabers and Lhanbryde ward in Moray. He was not elected.

Jim Stephen retired from Grampian Police in 2009. At that time he held the rank of Assistant Chief Constable. The lengthy Grampian Police investigation into Arlene Fraser's disappearance cost well over two million pounds. To date, the various trials and appeals in this case have cost the Scottish taxpayer more than half a million pounds in legal aid bills. No-one knows what the final bill is likely to be.

Conclusion

Did Nat Fraser arrange to have his wife Arlene killed in April 1998? Common-sense suggests that he most probably did. He had acted so violently towards her just a few weeks before that he had almost killed her and no-one else has been shown to have had any credible motive for wishing Arlene dead. If we use the legal notion of Cui Bono *("for whose benefit")*, the most basic way to examine the motives behind any crime, Nat Fraser tops the list - he had several pressing reasons to want his wife permanently out of the way.

The contention that she may not actually be dead at all but that she ran away from her children, her family and her friends seems to me to be entirely without merit and to be unsupported by any shred of credible evidence.

The British justice system is not predicated upon the application of common-sense. It is supposedly based on the provision of proof, and that is something that was notably lacking in both Nat Fraser's murder trials.

At the first trial, there was the issue of the rings. There can now be no doubt that these must have been removed from the house on Smith Street before the police video was made on 29th April 1998 by a member (or members) or Grampian

Police for reasons that are unknown. They must later have been replaced by a member (or members) of the same organization. When the significance of the absence and return of these rings later became a central part of the prosecution case against Nat Fraser, there were members of Grampian Police who knew this to be entirely inaccurate but who chose to say nothing in order to ensure that Fraser was convicted. At Nat Fraser's appeal hearing, his QC defined this as displaying *"an extraordinary degree of incompetence"*. This seems to me to be a very charitable description. There have been persistent claims that the rings were in the desk of a senior police officer while they were missing from the house, but this has never been proved. At the very least, this was not Grampian Police's finest hour.

It has also been said that Grampian Police adopted Nat Fraser as their main and only suspect almost as soon as the investigation began, meaning that they focused on collecting evidence to support this idea rather than looking more widely for other possible suspects. There may be some merit to this argument, but the fact is that Nat Fraser was always the main and only suspect in the disappearance of Arlene, so Grampian Police can hardly be faulted for vigorously pursuing this line of enquiry.

At both trials, there was the confused and confusing

testimony of Hector Dick. Hector Dick lied consistently to police about his role in purchasing the mysterious Ford Fiesta and again while under oath at the first four days during his trial for perverting the course of justice in 2001 – he only began to tell the truth at that trial when faced with the knowledge that the jury were about to see a video of him admitting buying the car. He then went on to explain that the purchase of the car had nothing to do with the disappearance of Arlene Fraser. However, at Nat Fraser's trial for murder in 2003 he told the jury under oath that the car _had_ been bought on behalf of Nat Fraser and probably used in the abduction of Arlene Fraser. Both these statements given under oath cannot be true, so we know that Dick was guilty of perjury on at least one occasion.

Then there was the transparent unfairness of the second trial. The first trial and its verdict were very widely reported in Scotland. This was followed by lurid press reporting based on the transcripts prepared by Jessica Rees which seemed to prove that Nat Fraser had been recorded discussing dismembering his wife's body. The fact that this transcript and Ms Rees professional reputation were subsequently seriously questioned did not receive the same level of press coverage and, when Nat Fraser was brought back to trial in 2012, none of the people selected as members of the jury could have been unaware of his previous conviction or the press reporting that followed. In that sense, it was never going to be possible to give Nat Fraser a fair second trial – Nat Fraser blamed the *"Google factor"* for his second conviction, correctly claiming that there was nothing to prevent members of the jury looking up details of his previous convictions. It was also notable that, other than the highly suspect testimony of Hector Dick, no direct evidence against Nat Fraser was produced at the second trial – all the evidence produced in court was circumstantial and based on inference and supposition.

In his first trial, Nat Fraser was found guilty partly on the basis of withheld evidence. In the second trial he faced public opinion which overwhelmingly considered him to be guilty before the trial began. In both trials he was convicted partly on the basis of testimony from a man who was known to lie under oath. Taking all these things together, Nat Fraser might reasonably claim that he has never received a fair trial. Despite this, I believe that the available evidence strongly suggests that both guilty verdicts were correct and that Nat Fraser is guilty of arranging Arlene's murder and deserves the life sentence he is currently serving.

It must also be said that if Nat Fraser was indeed implicated in his wife's murder, it is also true that he was the victim of catastrophically bad timing. Police forces are often unwilling to allocate scarce resources to look for missing people. The number of people who simply disappear in the UK every year is staggering – on average, well over 200,000 British people are reported missing annually. The vast majority of these people reappear in time, though anything up to 20,000 people stay missing for one year or more. Sadly, some of these people are probably dead – coroners' offices in the UK typically have a total of 1,000 unidentified and unclaimed bodies at any one time.

When an adult who is not known to have mental health issues vanishes and where there is no physical evidence to suggest foul play, the police response is often cursory even when there is no known reason for that person to disappear. Nat Fraser may have assumed that police interest in Arlene's disappearance would not last long. He could not have anticipated that continuing outrage over the Scott Simpson case would lead to the resignation of the Chief Constable just days before Arlene disappeared. Whatever else they might do, in April 1998 Grampian Police were not going to take the chance of being vilified again for failing to take a missing person case seriously.

Then there is the question of who actually abducted and killed Arlene, because Fraser's alibi makes it certain that this could not have been him? It is not possible to be completely certain about this, but there is one very notable suspect. Hector Dick was involved in the drink smuggling racket with Nat Fraser and stood to lose just as much as Nat if this were to be revealed. Hector Dick bought the mysterious beige Ford Fiesta and claimed under oath that he had taken it to a scrap yard in Elgin. The manager of the scrap yard was adamant that Dick was lying and gave police a lengthy statement about this. Hector Dick admitted that he has been burying old cars on his farm since the 1960s, but there does not appear to have been any attempt to discover whether he also buried the beige Fiesta there.

During Nat Fraser's first trial, a witness told the court that, around one week before she disappeared, Arlene had said that she was nervous because she had spotted Hector Dick sitting outside her house in a car for one hour. The defence suggested that this was Dick making a reconnaissance before returning to murder Arlene the following week. Dick claimed that he was there because Nat had asked him to pick up rubbish from the garden and dump it, a claim that Nat Fraser's solicitor called *"a preposterous, unbelievable pack of lies"*.

Most accounts of this case include the contention that Nat Fraser hired a *'hit-man'* to kill his wife, most probably someone from outside the local area. When you examine the background to this idea, it can be traced directly to several different statements given by Hector Dick, both in court and in his exclusive revelations to newspapers. The idea that an un-named hit-man was used originates solely with Dick, but perhaps Hecky had a very particular reason for wishing to focus the search for Arlene's killer outside the Elgin area?

So, Hector Dick certainly had the motive, means and opportunity to abduct and murder Arlene Fraser (while Nat Fraser has an alibi for the time of Arlene's disappearance, Hector Dick does not). Hector Dick lied repeatedly about his involvement both to the police and in court. Hector Dick was seen hanging around outside the bungalow on Smith Street less than one week before Arlene disappeared. Two witnesses claim that they called the Crime Stoppers telephone line to report that they had seen Hector Dick driving in his Land Rover on Smith Street on the morning of 28th April 1998 (though not parked outside Number 2). These witnesses say that they were never interviewed by the police. Hector Dick purchased the car which the police claim was used in Arlene's abduction, paying the seller extra in exchange for an agreement that he wouldn't tell anyone about the transaction. Then he disposed of the car, though we don't know where or how as he lied about this in court. Hector Dick had on his farm two large steam cookers which were capable of rendering whole cattle into pig feed.

Hector Dick was originally charged with Arlene's murder and this charge was only dropped when Dick agreed to testify against Nat Fraser. Many people are very uneasy about the fact that Dick only agreed to testify in return for the dropping of a demand for £250,000 by HMRC. A fine on this scale would have ruined Dick and this certainly gave him a powerful incentive to tell the court what the police wanted to hear. Some people have even said that this sounds rather like a bribe, though if it were to be regarded in that way it would of course invalidate all the testimony that Dick has given about this case.

The main testimony against Nat Fraser at both trials has come from Hector Dick. Unlike Glenn Lucas, Hector Dick has never offered to take a lie detector test about his role in Arlene's disappearance. Arlene's family continue to believe that Hector Dick was involved in Arlene's disappearance and some of them believe that he was her murderer. Most people who regard him as guilty assume that Dick abducted and killed Arlene at the instigation of Nat Fraser and probably because he was paid to do so. There are still a few people who claim that Fraser had nothing to do with the murder and that it was entirely Dick's idea.

The role of Ian Taylor is also not entirely clear. Initially, he claimed to have been convinced that his friend and business partner was innocent, but that after his conviction and the release of the transcript by Jessica Rees he came to accept that Nat was guilty and decided to have nothing further to do with him. Taylor gave an interview to the Sunday Mail newspaper in 2005 in which he claimed that Nat Fraser told him that Arlene was killed using chloroform and her body wrapped in plastic sheeting before it was taken out of the house (he also claimed in the same interview that he had seen both chloroform and plastic sheeting in Hector Dick's Land Rover). Nat Fraser could only have told him this before the first trial (because Taylor had no contact with him after he was convicted) so Taylor's claim that he believed in Fraser's innocence up to that point can't be true. Taylor was charged with four firearm offences in 1999 relating to shotguns he possessed without valid certificates, though it was never suggested that these had any connection with Arlene's disappearance.

I must also mention the beige Ford Fiesta which flits in and out of this story like a will-o'-the-wisp. After interviewing Kevin Ritchie about the sale of this car to Hector Dick, Grampian Police became convinced that it had been involved in the abduction and murder of Arlene. Let's just think about that for a moment. One would imagine that, if a hit-man wanted a car to be used during a murder and the disposal of a body, the most basic pre-requisite would be a vehicle with a boot, so that the body could be transported out of sight. But the Ford Fiesta is a small hatchback – it doesn't have a boot. It does have a small luggage compartment behind the rear seats, but on this particular Fiesta the rear parcel shelf was missing, so that anything placed in that area would be clearly visible from outside.

Kevin Ritchie also told the police that the car was fitted with a *"Cherry Bomb"* exhaust – a very loud aftermarket exhaust. This would attract attention to the car wherever it was driven. It would be difficult to imagine any vehicle less suited to the needs of an assassin and I cannot help feeling that the beige Fiesta is actually a red herring which was most probably purchased by Hector Dick to be used in the drink smuggling racket. I believe that his later accounts of the car being used as part of Arlene's abduction were invented because that is what he believed Grampian Police wanted him to say.

Then there are the physical circumstances of Arlene's disappearance. Smith Street in New Elgin is a narrow but busy street within a small community. People notice who is going where and when. Arlene was seen on the two occasions when she briefly left the house (once to hang out washing and once to wave to her children) on the morning of 28th April 1998. Yet we have to believe that in the middle of the morning, one or more people parked outside the house (it didn't have a garage or anywhere out of sight to park), walked up to the front door, were admitted then returned a short time later carrying the body of Arlene

Fraser, placed this in the vehicle and drove off. Without anyone noticing anything at all? If you add to this the possibility that the abductor was using the Ford Fiesta with a very noisy exhaust then the chances of this going unnoticed fall to zero.

For these reasons, I think that the generally accepted scenario that Arlene was abducted from Number 2 Smith Street may be wrong. Less than thirty meters from the front door of the house, Smith Street joins the A941 (also known as Main Street), the main route into Elgin from the south and the town of Rothes. Near the junction of Smith Street and Main Street is a small shop. It would take just moments to walk from the bungalow on Smith Street to the shop on Main Street. I believe it is more likely that Arlene suddenly realized that there was something she urgently needed from the shop, perhaps something required for her lunch date with Michele Scott? I think that she put on her favorite brown coat and went out to go to the shop. I have never understood why the coat was missing unless Arlene put it on herself – if you were looking for something in which to wrap a body, you'd use a sheet or duvet, something that would completely conceal the body, not a coat.

We know that she never arrived at the shop. Instead, I believe that someone stopped as she was walking along Smith Street and she got into their vehicle before she reached the shop. I believe that person was on their way to Smith Street to abduct and/or murder Arlene when they met her in the street by chance. Somehow, they persuaded her to get into their vehicle where she was incapacitated or murdered at once. I believe this explains not just the missing coat but the complete absence of sightings of a vehicle outside Number 2 Smith Street at the relevant time. It also means that the driver of the vehicle would have to be someone Arlene knew – she would never have got into a car with a complete stranger. Two witnesses claimed to have seen Hector Dick driving on Smith Street on the morning of 28th April 1998, though neither were ever interviewed by the police.

When Grampian Police agreed a deal with Hector Dick during the first murder trial in 2003, I think they did this with the best of intentions – without Dick's testimony, the chances of convicting Nat Fraser seemed slim. By granting Dick immunity from prosecution for the murder of Arlene Fraser in return for his turning Queen's Evidence, I suspect that they may also have inadvertently protected someone who would later become a prime suspect.

With all the focus on trials, testimony, Nat Fraser, Hector Dick, Glenn Lucas, Grampian Police and the missing Ford Fiesta, it's easy to lose sight of the person that this story is really about: Arlene Fraser. There are a number of websites and forums where there is a great deal of discussion about whether Nat Fraser has received justice from the Scottish legal system. I can understand that debate. I might even agree with parts of it. But I think we can be quite certain that Arlene Fraser was given no justice at all. She wasn't a saint, but from all accounts she was a loving mother and a vibrant, vivacious and intelligent young woman who had put in place plans to improve her situation. The available evidence strongly suggests that those plans and her life were brutally cut short on the morning of 28th April 1998.

I would love to believe that Arlene Fraser escaped her increasingly frightening and unstable existence in Elgin in 1998 and fled to a better, safer life in the sun. I would love to believe that, but I cannot. The evidence overwhelmingly suggests that Arlene Fraser is dead and that she was abducted and murdered on April 28th by a person or persons presently officially unknown and at the instigation of her violent, jealous and conniving husband. It seems unlikely in the present circumstances, but I hope that one day her murderer will be brought to justice so that her children, family and friends may finally achieve closure and find out what happened to her.

I hope you enjoyed reading this book. If you did, please take a moment to leave me a review on Amazon. Your opinion matters and positive reviews help me greatly. Thank you.

I welcome feedback from readers. If you have comments on this book or ideas for other books in the Murder World series, please send me an email at: stevemac357@gmail.com.

About the Author

Steve is a Scot who writes non-fiction on a range of topics including true crime and the paranormal. He has been interested in crime writing since he read his first true crime book, in secret, at the local library in 1971, when everyone thought he was studying for his homework. Now he doesn't have to do it in secret anymore and reads a range of work by various crime writers.

He is married with two grown-up children and currently lives in Andalucía in Spain.

Other Murder World Scotland books

If you enjoyed this book, you may also be interested in these other Murder World Scotland Books which are also available on Amazon:

The Butler's Story: The extraordinary life and crimes of Archibald Thomson Hall

Archibald Thompson Hall was a complicated man. A bisexual born in the working-class back streets of Glasgow, he craved culture and the finer things in life. Sadly, his life hadn't equipped him with the means to obtain these so he stole them instead. He worked as a burglar, thief and con-man for many years before stumbling on a role that suited him well – he became a butler and transformed himself into the urbane, charming and imperturbable gentleman's gentleman Roy Fontaine.

Working as a butler certainly gave him opportunities to steal and embezzle from his employers, but it also led him to face arrest, conviction and prison on more than one occasion (though he became the first person to escape from one of Britain's first high-security prisons). It wasn't until 1977, when he was fifty-three, that he finally discovered his true vocation as a murderer. He committed his first murder in November 1977 and by January the following year he had killed five people and would almost certainly have gone on to kill many more if he hadn't been caught.

This is the true story of a charming, charismatic, intelligent, entertaining, cold, ruthless and merciless killer and one of the most dangerous men in the annals of Scottish crime.

A killing at kinky cottage: The murder of Max Garvie

The Swinging sixties eventually reached even the tranquil Howe O' the Mearns in the North-East of Scotland. Millionaire farmer Max Garvie and his glamorous wife Sheila became so well-known for their nudist and sex parties that their farmhouse became known locally as *'kinky cottage.'*

However, beneath the swinging exterior, all was not well in the marriage of Max and Sheila. Max was easily bored and constantly sought new sexual adventures and partners. Sheila was interested in a more stable and lasting relationship, but not with Max.

Then, one evening in May 1968, the peace and quiet of this tranquil farming community was ripped apart by a shotgun blast. It seemed that Sheila had finally found a permanent way to solve her marital problems. But was it really that simple?

The Vanishing: The Renee MacRae case

One November evening in 1976, Renee MacRae, the estranged wife of a millionaire Scottish businessman, set off from her luxury home in Inverness. She was going, she had told her husband, to spend the weekend with her sister in Kilmarnock and she took her three year old son Andrew with her.

Four hours later her BMW car was found burning in a remote lay-by on the A9, the main road to the south from Inverness. In the car there was no sign of Renee, Andrew or their luggage.

Police enquiries quickly discovered that Renee's real reason for leaving Inverness was very different to the story she had told her estranged husband and discovered that her life was rather more complicated than it appeared from the outside. The search for the missing mother and son was huge and this became the longest running missing person investigation in Scottish history. Despite this, no trace of Renee or Andrew was ever found.

Officially, Renee MacRae is still missing and no-one has

ever been charged with her murder or that of her son. However, over the forty years that have passed since she vanished, tantalizing clues have emerged that allow us to consider the various theories, to work out the most likely course of events that November night and to identify the person most likely to have caused the disappearance.

The face of Bible John: The search for a Scottish serial killer

Just like any other country, Scotland has its share of unsolved crimes. However, few have proved to be as enduringly fascinating as the story of the man who became known as Bible John and who killed at least three women in Glasgow in the late 1960s.

This murderer picked up each of his three known victims at the Barrowland Ballroom in the east of the city centre. The bodies of all three women were later found dumped. All three were mothers, all had been menstruating at the time of their death and all were beaten, raped and strangled. In each case, pieces of the women's clothing vanished.

The murderer made no attempt to conceal or disguise himself and was seen by a number of witnesses at the ballroom and outside - one witness actually shared a taxi with the killer and one of his victims. Through discussions with these witnesses, a well-known artist working on behalf of the police produced a striking portrait of a man with red hair and blue/grey eyes and wearing a cold, rather supercilious expression. This portrait was widely publicized and became known as the face of Bible John. People wondered how the man could possibly avoid arrest with his likeness on the front of every major Scottish newspaper and on police posters throughout the city?

How was this be possible? The murderer frequented a busy public place and was seen with all his victims by a number of witnesses who got a good look at him. By the time of the third murder, there had been massive publicity and people were on their guard and actually looking for a potential killer. Given that, just how did this person manage to kill three times and yet still escape detection? Having killed three times, why did he stop? Did he really stop at all or did he just become more adept at hiding his crimes? Perhaps most importantly of all, did Bible John really exist at all or was he nothing more than an urban myth?

Made in the USA
Columbia, SC
25 November 2023